Business and the Natural Environment

The fields of corporate environmentalism, green business and corporate sustainability have grown significantly over the past 25 years, such that the academic research domains of business decision-making, accounting, organizational behavior and the protection of the natural environment have developed into maturing areas of study within the management sciences.

Business and the Natural Environment: A Research Overview is a summary of the research thus far on this topic, offering a structure for understanding its emergence and growth, the multiple facets that make up its present state and a glimpse into the future of where it may be going. Along the way, the authors provide a compendium of its important works to help situate the interested reader in the landscape of the field. One important element of this work is its topical relevance; issues of environmental protection (and more recently sustainability) are critically important in today's worlds of business, policy and public understanding. Scholars who choose to enter this domain have much to offer of societal value while at the same time, entering a non-fully legitimate research stream that can lead to academic success (such as tenure).

This shortform book provides a research map for both new scholars who wish to enter the field and more seasoned researchers who wish to understand one view of the landscape and how they might fit within it. This expert survey of the existing literature brings the research story into the age of the Anthropocene and is essential primary reading.

Andrew J. Hoffman is the Holcim (US) Professor of Sustainable Enterprise at the University of Michigan, a position that holds joint appointments in the Management & Organizations department at the Stephen M. Ross School of Business and the Sustainable Systems group at the School of Environment and Sustainability. He has published over 100 articles/book chapters, as well as 14 books, which have been translated into six languages. In this work, he focuses on the processes by which environmental issues both emerge and evolve as social, political and managerial issues. He received his joint PhD in Management and Civil & Environmental Engineering at the Massachusetts Institute of Technology.

Susse Georg is Professor of Sustainable Innovation at the University of Aalborg, Copenhagen campus, in Denmark. Prior to her appointment at Aalborg University in 2012, she held a professorship at Copenhagen Business School and was co-director for CBS' research platform on "Sustainable Business." She has published articles, book chapters and two books on the development of corporate environmental management, clean technologies and sustainable cities. She is currently researching the organizational and institutional changes necessary for increased use of intermittent renewable energy in smart energy systems. She received her PhD in Environmental Economics and Policy from Copenhagen Business School.

State of the Art in Business Research
Edited by Professor Geoffrey Wood

Recent advances in theory, methods and applied knowledge (alongside structural changes in the global economic ecosystem) have presented researchers with challenges in seeking to stay abreast of their fields and navigate new scholarly terrains.

State of the Art in Business Research presents shortform books which provide an expert map to guide readers through new and rapidly evolving areas of research. Each title will provide an overview of the area, a guide to the key literature and theories and time-saving summaries of how theory interacts with practice.

As a collection, these books provide a library of theoretical and conceptual insights, and exposure to novel research tools and applied knowledge, that aid and facilitate in defining the state of the art, as a foundation stone for a new generation of research.

Print ISSN: 2575–4815
Online ISSN: 2575–4807

Innovation Management
A Research Overview
Mark Dodgson

Business and the Natural Environment
A Research Overview
Andrew Hoffman and Susse Georg

Business and the Natural Environment

A Research Overview

**Andrew J. Hoffman and
Susse Georg**

LONDON AND NEW YORK

First published 2018
by Routledge
2 Park Square, Milton Park, Abingdon, Oxon OX14 4RN

and by Routledge
711 Third Avenue, New York, NY 10017

Routledge is an imprint of the Taylor & Francis Group, an informa business

© 2018 Andrew J. Hoffman and Susse Georg

British Library Cataloguing-in-Publication Data
A catalogue record for this book is available from the British Library

Library of Congress Cataloging-in-Publication Data
A catalog record for this book has been requested

ISBN: 978-0-8153-7582-1 (hbk)
ISBN: 978-1-351-23894-6 (ebk)

Typeset in Times New Roman
by Apex CoVantage, LLC

Contents

Figures

Acknowledgments

We wish to thank the folks at Routledge for their support of this book as well as of our 2013 Four Volume set: *Business and the Environment: Critical Perspectives in Business and Management*. In particular, we would like to thank Terry Clague, Senior Publisher, for his assistance on this book and Simon Alexander, Senior Development Editor, for assistance on the last one. These two books are closely intertwined as we used a great deal of material from the introduction to that earlier (and rather large) volume as a foundation upon which to build the chapters in this book. By adding additional and updated material and expanding our assessment to consider the future directions of the field, we hope this new and more condensed version will prove useful to new scholars as they enter the field, and senior scholars as they ponder the landscape of the field and their place within it. Lastly, we would like to acknowledge and thank each other on this book. We have each enjoyed our collaborations and each of us has contributed equally to creating this manuscript.

Andrew J. Hoffman, Ann Arbor, Michigan, USA
Susse Georg, Copenhagen, Denmark

1 Introduction

Every field of inquiry goes through a life cycle; a new idea emerges, it develops into a growing body of literature and either continues to grow or enters into decline (Downs, 1972). A sure sign of the successful growth of a field is an effort to institutionalize its history, categorize its accomplishments and project its future directions. The field of Business and the Natural Environment (B&NE) has reached that stage. After expanding in the early 1990s as a distinct field of empirical inquiry, it has grown to include contributions from the full gamut of business disciplines. By 2010, the field had matured and interest (as measured by article counts and society membership) had reached a plateau. Looking forward, there are new issues and new topics that the field will embrace as it progresses in the coming decades.

This book provides a brief overview of the trajectories of the field's development, offering a structure for understanding its emergence and growth, the multiple facets that make up its present state and a glimpse into the future of where it may be going. Along the way, we will provide a compendium of its important works to help situate the interested reader in the landscape of the field. One important element of this work is its topical relevance; issues of environmental protection – and more recently sustainability – are critically important in today's worlds of business, policy and public understanding. Scholars who choose to enter this domain have much to offer of societal value.

The B&NE field emerged as a response to calls over the last 40 years for the corporate sector to minimize resource use, reduce pollution and prevent damage to the environment. Despite some progress, many of these problems continue to persist, and new and grave problems have surfaced. These problems include climate change, water scarcity, toxic waste, habitat destruction, species extinction and many other issues that are directly related to the ways our market systems provide society with food, buildings, energy, transport, mobility, clothing, synthetic chemicals and other material aspects of our modern culture. In each of these domains business is heavily implicated, both as part of the problem and as part of the solution. B&NE scholars have sought to uncover the deeper elements of what drives companies to address these issues, the organizational and technical structures they develop to respond to them, and the resultant innovations that emerge to transform organizational and market systems.

Although a few authors started addressing the environmental problems associated with corporate production and consumption patterns as early as the beginning of the twentieth century, it was not until the mid-1990s that B&NE scholars began to vigorously engage in an analysis of business responses to environmental concerns. Some of this early work emerged in the broader and older field of corporate social responsibility (CSR) (Aguilera et al., 2007; Carroll, 1979; Matten and Crane, 2005; Matten and Moon, 2008). But given that environmental pollution and protection lent itself more readily to clear and distinct quantification, regulation and theorization, the B&NE field found itself able to connect to existing paradigms of shareholder capitalism and regulatory control, and therefore carve itself out as a separate (but related) domain.

While some continue to use the notions of B&NE and CSR interchangeably, others make the clear distinction between the two with CSR placing more emphasis on the philanthropic, social and less quantifiable aspects of business practice (e.g. anti-corruption, philanthropy to support local endeavors, etc.) and B&NE denoting quantitative damages to the natural environment (e.g. CO_2 emissions, toxic discharges, waste, water and energy use, etc.). Some associate CSR more with multi-national corporations (MNCs) than small to medium sized enterprises (SMEs), but there is a growing interest in how SMEs are grappling with these issues (Ángel del Brio and Junquera, 2003; Hilary, 2004; Petts et al., 1999). Some scholars have also entered this domain through the area of family business (Sharma, 2004). Others emphasize the difference between the US and European approaches to CSR. According to Matten and Moon (2008), CSR in the US is more likely to be the result of corporate discretion (which they label "explicit CSR"), whereas CSR in European corporations seeks to address stakeholder issues and exhibit proper obligations in keeping with societal expectations ("implicit CSR"). This transatlantic difference is mainly attributed to differences in the institutional framework and underlying societal norms, values and expectations (Matten and Moon, 2008).

Some bemoan the lack of a precise definition for both CSR and B&NE, but in seeking strict, consistent definitions there is a risk of "overlooking" the contested nature of these issues (Macnaghten and Urry, 1998) and, more importantly, glossing over the complexities, uncertainties and ambiguities that both domains entail. There is, however, an equal danger that too much interpretive flexibility may blind scholars (in the eyes of some, such as Gladwin, 2012) to the challenges of changing corporate behavior and to the complex contingencies of "success" (less environmentally damaging behavior while increasing profits). Indeed, as ecological challenges continue to grow (despite more than 40 years of efforts to redress them), both CSR and B&NE will continue to be of great importance, even as strict definitions remain difficult to uphold. Moreover, the entanglement of the social and environmental domains is captured in the extant conceptions of corporate sustainability (Ehrenfeld, 2008; Elkington, 1999) and its associated rubric of the triple bottom line that accounts for a company's environmental, social and economic performance. Nevertheless, B&NE has remained a distinct and autonomous field which has passed through and encompassed multiple iterations: empirically, theoretically, conceptually and geographically.

Empirically, the focus has considered media-based issues of water, air and land based pollutants in a variety of different industries, and moved from end of pipe solutions to clean technologies, the introduction of management system tools (ISO, EMAS etc.), the greening of the supply chains and others issues.

Theoretically, scholars have approached these issues through the lenses of existing business disciplines regarding organizational behavior, corporate strategy, marketing, operations, accounting and finance, and augmented these perspectives with further insights from economics, sociology, psychology and political science. In a few rare instances, some have attempted to link to the natural sciences (Starik, 1995; Whiteman, Walker and Perego, 2013). It is a field characterized by the use of multiple interpretive frameworks.

Conceptually, the relationship between business and the natural environment has been characterized in multiple ways. Some characterize the phenomena of environmental management as a linear evolution of stages in the corporate development process, with companies moving up the ladder of environmentalism (Hoffman and Ehrenfeld, 1998; 2015; Hunt and Auster, 1990). Some problematize this phenomena as an ongoing battle waged among competing interests and social movements, with its requisite ebbs and flows. Some consider environmental management as a means for continual internalization of environmental externalities, with policies playing a critical role in either curbing environmental insults through coercive command and control policies or incentivizing better corporate behavior through market-based policies. In both cases, the focus is on monetizing environmental insults. Some see a darker side to corporate environmentalism as power-plays, green-washing and regulatory capture (Lyon and Maxwell, 2011). And finally, some see corporations as the solution to environmental problems as they innovatively respond to evolving markets and changing institutional and political environments (Hoffman, 2001a).

Geographically, the B&NE field is a multi-national field, growing largely in North America and Europe. More recently, Asian and Australasian scholars have entered the field, adding important insights on environmental issues associated with their growing industrial base. While B&NE research in North America and Europe emerged around the same time and grew in unison, there are differences with regard to the topics addressed and the theoretical and methodological approaches used. North American scholarship has tended to emphasize the theoretical focus of the disciplinary management journals and directed its inquiry at academic colleagues in those disciplinary fields. European scholarship, on the other hand, has tended to draw upon (newer) social theories such as critical management theory, practice theory and actor-network theory. It has a stronger emphasis on qualitative studies and has been published more in specialized journals. Engaging with audiences within the corporate community is the aim of much research across the continents (though, many would argue not enough). Today, the North American, European, Asian and Australiasian fields are finding more interconnections as the journals, conferences and norms of doctoral training and academic publishing begin to merge. Such a merging of these research traditions serves to further institutionalize the field, normalize its scope, expand its volume and create a rich foundation of literature upon which to build future inquiry. This work has been increasingly published in mainstream "A" journals but also continues to flourish within specialized journals that allow deviation from the strict norms of theoretical orthodoxy.

In short, the field of B&NE is a wide-ranging one that has grown to now include various empirical foci, theoretical disciplines, conceptualized models and geographic traditions. Each component offers a different piece of the composite whole for understanding how and why environmental issues impact and are impacted by the corporate system. More importantly, this literature has now reached a stage where it has sufficient critical mass and intellectual rigor that it has gained the legitimacy of not only fitting within, but also augmenting and improving, the existing paradigms of academic literature. At the same time, the field has maintained some of its more provocative roots by honoring on-going critical analyses that challenge those existing paradigms (Bansal and Gao, 2006; Bansal and Hoffman, 2012; Georg and Hoffman, 2013; Gladwin, 1993; Shrivastava, 1994; Kallio and Nordberg, 2006).

But this growing legitimacy raises questions about the present state of the field and its future trajectory. In light of its history, B&NE research can hardly be said to represent one stream of discussion, but what are the streams and sub-streams? Are the debates and discussions that make up the B&NE domain best represented as one large interconnected discourse, many individual and isolated conversations, or a combination in which some articles bridge disciplines? And even further, how does this domain of scholarship fit with the rest of the work within the management literature? Is B&NE research a field of study that informs other management domains or is it an isolated domain onto itself? And finally, how do we make sense of the fact the corpus of B&NE research is not leading to an alleviation of the environmental problems that motivate it? Issues of climate change, water scarcity, species extinction and other issues continue to worsen (Ehrenfeld and Hoffman, 2013; Rockström et al., 2009). In short, how do we characterize the purpose and success of the B&NE research domain as a composite whole?

Answering these questions is one goal of this research monograph. We also hope to offer a view of the field that may allow B&NE scholars to understand the overall landscape as well as its various contours. At the same time, we hope to stimulate reflection and debate over the state of the field of B&NE scholarship and where it might or should be going. To that end, we do not offer the definitive final word, but rather a perspective and commentary upon which we hope others will build. At this time in the history of B&NE research, we have an opportunity to explore the ways in which corporate practice has been studied and theorized as a backdrop for thinking about renewed ways in which it could be studied and amended. It is important for the training of new scholars who enter the domain to periodically take stock of where senior scholars have laid the field's foundations. (We refer to "senior" scholars with some amusement; as B&NE is in fact a relatively new field, where the senior members within it are relatively young – at least in our eyes! – compared to what we traditionally consider to be more mature and established fields.) But again, a question that this point raises is whether B&NE being characterized as a "young" field is due to a lack of a shared (specialized) conceptual frameworks and standardized research methods or a vibrancy that comes from addressing some of society's grand challenges and allows it to avoid the inertia of a long historical legacy. Finally, it is important that this review of B&NE research remain closely linked to the natural worlds as studied by the natural sciences so as to maintain its focus on the state the latter by studying advances in the former. The fraying of this linkage will be discussed in more depth in chapter 4.

The remainder of this book comprises three chapters and a conclusion. Chapter 2 offers a history of publications during the development of the field in 1990s and 2000s; presenting a statistical synopsis of when papers have been published, where and with what focus, as well as a network analysis map to depict the form and flow of its multiple conversations. Chapter 3 highlights the main conversations taking place in the field today, emphasizing how the various conversations cluster and interconnect and highlighting the major papers that inform those discussions. Chapter 4 considers the future of the field, particularly as it relates to the emerging awareness that we and entering a new reality which geo-scientists call the Anthropocene.

Viewed from this perspective, much of the research that B&NE scholars produce may have limited bearing on the worsening state of the environment. Chapter 5 offers some concluding remarks for the reader's consideration as they ponder the state of the B&NE field. These chapters provide the basic groundwork for understanding the structure, nature, history and trajectory of the B&NE field, one that will be entertaining for the experienced scholars who have lived it with us, and informative for the novice scholar who wishes to take the challenge of continuing the field into the future.

2 Contours of an emerging field

Historical development of B&NE research

An obvious way to study the scientific discourse within a field is to examine what has been published. Based on a sample of 874 major articles in B&NE between 1975 and 2010,[1] this chapter maps key features of the field in terms of number of publications, types of outlets, citation patterns. As we can see in figure 2.1 (Hoffman, 2011a), the historical trajectory of the number of these scientific B&NE articles published per year shows that B&NE research dates back to before the early 1970s, but did not fully begin to develop as a substantial body of literature until the early 1990s. It has grown at a steady rate until around 2010 (Hoffman, 2011c), where it appears to have plateaued. Seventy-three percent of these articles were published in mainstream academic journals (non-specialized), while

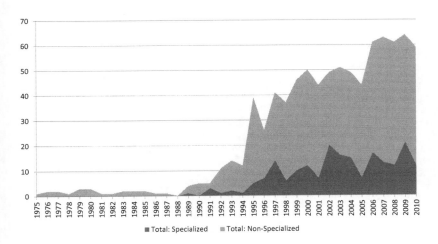

Figure 2.1 Articles per year on B&NE, 1975–2010

27% were published in journals that focus specifically on environmental issues in a particular discipline.

The coalescence of the field in the early 1990s coincides with a convergence in salience and attention for environmental issues as *strategic* concerns within the business community, as addressed in the "second wave" of business sustainability illustrated in figure 2.2 (Hoffman and Ehrenfeld, 2015). The first wave, beginning in the 1970s, dominated by a focus on policies to reduce environmental pollution, brought environmental issues to corporate attention as a matter of regulatory compliance. But the second wave, beginning in the 1990s, reframed the issue as one of corporate strategy (Hoffman, 2001a). The third wave began in the first decade of the twenty-first century and is characterized by a more encompassing approach that introduces social issues to the mix of environmental concerns as companies attend to the triple bottom line of sustainability. The fourth wave, which we are presently entering, represents a shift towards recognition that we have entered the Anthropocene, a new geologic epoch in which humans are an animating force within the environment. Each of these waves exands the domain of B&NE research, each being layered on top of the wave that preceded it.

Movement through these waves can be described as moving through a series of transitions from normal to revolutionary science (Kuhn, 1970). A phase of normal science begins when a theory emerges as dominant to other existing theories and becomes the "paradigm." But, established theories become challenged and ultimately change when anomalous events

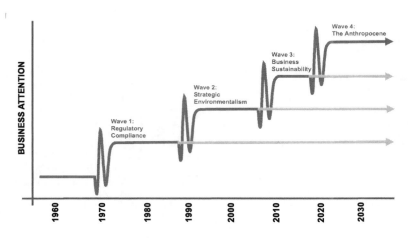

Figure 2.2 The four "waves" of business sustainability

emerge which cannot be explained or solved by the existing order. Conflict over the nature, meaning and response to these events ensues, and the period of revolutionary science ends when a new theory is successful in providing a socially adequate response to the anomaly and becomes the basis of the new paradigm.

We can view the shifting beliefs around corporate environmentalism as having been precipitated by such periods of punctuated equilibrium (Gersick, 1991). The advent of the first wave was triggered by events such as Rachel Carson's book *Silent Spring* in 1962, the Santa Barbara oil spill in 1969, the Cuyahoga River Fire in 1969, the growing number of problems associated with the dumping of toxic wastes in landfills across Europe and the drying out of the Aral lake in the former Soviet Union, which led to the formation of national environmental agencies and regulations both in the United States (Hoffman, 2001a) and Europe (Jamison, Eyerman and Cramer, 1990) in the early 1970s.

The second wave was triggered by events such as the Seveso disaster in 1976, the Bhopal Disaster of 1984, the discovery of the Arctic ozone hole in 1985, the Sandoz spill of toxic chemicals into the Rhine river in 1986, the Chernobyl nuclear disaster in 1986, and the Exxon Valdez oil spill in 1990, which elevated pollution concerns to a new, more regional and global level and brought environmental issues into the mainstream of business in the 1990s through its integration with concerns from insurance companies, investors, consumers and competitors (Hoffman, 2001a). The third wave was propelled by a series of events that followed the creation of a global constituency for sustainable development created by the 1992 Summit of the UN Commission on Commerce and Development. This wave prompted a growing recognition of the importance of business in promoting sustainable developments in the face persistent and worsening environmental and associated social problems, and the limitations of governments in their ability to solve them (Kraemer and Gostin, 2012). We will reserve discussion of the fourth wave until chapter 4, which considers the future of the field.

Within the world of management research, the second wave in the 1990s marks a number of events that establish the B&NE field, and which were propelled forward in the third wave: the first gathering of management scholars on the topic at the Greening of Industry Network conference in 1989; the establishment of the Organizations and the Natural Environment (ONE) special interest group of the Academy of Management in 1994; and the establishment of specialized academic journals dedicated to the interface between managerial action and environmental protection, including *Organization & Environment* (started as *Industrial and Environmental*

Crisis Quarterly in 1987 and changed to *Organization & Environment* in 1997), *Business Strategy & the Environment* (started in 1992) and the *Journal of Industrial Ecology* (started in 1997).

The emergence of the field was also spurred on by a series of special issues on B&NE themes in multiple disciplinary journals, including: *Psychology & Marketing* (1994), *Academy of Management Review* (1995), *Journal of Advertising* (1995), *British Journal of Management* (1996), *American Behavioral Scientist* (1999), *Business History Review* (1999), *Academy of Management Journal* (2000), *Production and Operations Management* (2001) as well as books (Roome, 1998; Fischer and Schot, 1993). With this as a backdrop, B&NE research began to emerge in a broad spectrum of journals, both specialized and mainstream.

Journals in which B&NE research has been published

Our sample of 874 major B&NE articles were published in 258 journals and 85 book chapters (See Appendix I for a list of the journals). Of these articles, the majority (36%) was in the broad discipline of management, followed by accounting, economics and operations (see table 2.1). Notably low in research productivity were the disciplines of finance and information technology.

The mean number of articles per journal in the sample was 1, and the average was 2.91 meaning that a small number of journals published the bulk of the work. Specifically, 36 journals accounted for 56% of all articles

Table 2.1 Distribution of B&NE articles by discipline

Discipline	Articles	Percentage
Management	280	36
Accounting	90	12
Economics	74	10
Operations	56	7
Behavior: Psychology, Sociology, Org Behavior	50	6
Engineering/Science/Environment	47	6
Marketing	47	6
Political Science	47	6
Professional	45	6
Law	27	3
Finance	12	2
Information Systems	2	0

published and specialized journals made up 27% of the total scholarship. The journals that published the most B&NE research were the *Journal of Industrial Ecology, Academy of Management Journal, Business Strategy & the Environment, Strategic Management Journal, Academy of Management Review* and *Organization & Environment* (see table 2.2). Note that of the

Table 2.2 Distribution of B&NE articles by journal

Journal	Articles
Journal of Industrial Ecology	36
Academy of Management Journal	29
Business Strategy & the Environment	27
Academy of Management Review	25
Organization & Environment	25
Strategic Management Journal	25
Journal of Business Ethics	20
Accounting, Organizations and Society	19
Accounting, Auditing and Accountability Journal	17
Journal of Cleaner Production	17
Journal of Environmental Economics and Management	17
California Management Review	16
Greener Management International	15
Production and Operations Management	12
Harvard Business Review	10
Journal of Management Studies	10
Administrative Science Quarterly	9
Journal of Economics and Management Strategy	9
Management Science	9
Ecological Economics	8
Journal of Business Venturing	8
Organization Studies	8
Organization Science	7
Policy Sciences	7
Advances in Environmental Accounting and Management	6
Journal of Marketing	6
Journal of Operations Management	6
Sloan Management Review	6
Academy of Management Executive	5
Advances in Public Interest Accounting	5
American Behavioral Scientist	5
Corporate Governance	5
Corporate Social Responsibility and Environmental Management	5
European Accounting Review	5
Journal of Law and Economics	5

top 10 journals, four are non-specialized mainstream journals. Although B&NE research is visible in top journals, it does not figure prominently. A study by Bansal and Gao (2006) found that B&NE research figured in less than 1% of the research in mainstream journals, when a few special issues on the topic were taken out of the sample. Our study confirms that specialized journals continued to remain a prominent outlet for B&NE research.

Citation counts of B&NE research

It appears that the most influential articles, measured by citations per article in table 2.3 (gathered from Googlescholar©), came from B&NE research published in the professional journals by a wide margin. Citation counts per article ranged from 0 to 4,461 overall.[2] The average citation count per article was 130, but the median was 50 citations per article, suggesting that some articles at the top of the list skew the distribution.

More specifically, articles with the highest influence (measured by citation count per article) came from the *Academy of Management Review; Harvard Business Review; Academy of Management Journal; Journal of Marketing; Accounting, Auditing and Accountability Journal; Business & Society*; and *California Management Review*. These rankings do not appear to correlate with the journal's overall Impact Factor (see table 2.4).

Have B&NE scholars been publishing in the right outlets for maximum impact? The results seem to be mixed. Notice the mismatch between journals

Table 2.3 Citation counts of B&NE articles by discipline

Discipline	Citations/ Article
Professional	258.33
Economics	173.41
Engineering/Science	147.13
Management	146.75
Accounting	120.44
Finance	107.00
Law	105.33
Behavior: Psychology, Sociology, Org Behavior	96.40
Political Science	77.55
Operations	73.00
Marketing	68.17
Information Systems	18.50

Table 2.4 Citation count of B&NE articles by journal

Journal	Citations/ Article	Journal impact factor
Academy of Management Review	606.4	7.87
Harvard Business Review	481.9	1.66
Academy of Management Journal	267.3	6.48
Journal of Marketing	223.0	3.78
Accounting, Auditing and Accountability Journal	188.1	na
Business and Society	186.5	na
California Management Review	186.3	1.98
Management Science	182.9	2.23
Journal of Environmental Economics and Management	178.6	2.58
Accounting, Organizations and Society	173.6	1.90
Strategic Management Journal	169.4	4.46
Organization Studies	169.0	2.12
Sloan Management Review	145.7	1.14
Journal of Operations Management	129.0	3.24
Administrative Science Quarterly	125.3	3.84
Academy of Management Executive	120.4	na
Journal of Management Studies	115.9	2.81
Production and Operations Management	89.8	2.08
Journal of Law and Economics	87.0	1.64
Ecological Economics	78.1	2.42
European Accounting Review	71.7	0.96
Journal of Business Ethics	66.7	1.09
Journal of Cleaner Production	64.4	1.87
Business Strategy & the Environment	64.3	na
Journal of Economics and Management Strategy	62.8	1.24
Organization Science	62.4	3.13
Policy Sciences	61.0	0.73
Advances in Public Interest Accounting	52.6	na
Business Ethics Quarterly	51.3	1.62
Journal of Industrial Ecology	50.8	na
Policy Studies Journal	46.2	0.62
Advances in Environmental Accounting and Management	44.6	na
American Behavioral Scientist	30.8	0.71
Journal of Purchasing and Supply Management	30.0	na
Organization & Environment	27.0	1.07

listed in tables 2.2 and 2.4. For example, *Business & Society* received a high rank for citation/article but does not appear in the list of journals in which the research is published (only four articles were posted). Conversely, *Business Strategy & the Environment*, the *Journal of Industrial Ecology* and *Organization & Environment* were prominent outlets for B&NE research but receive very low ranks for citation counts. In between, *Academy of Management Review*, *Academy of Management Journal* and *Strategic Management Journal* rank comparably on both tables. Might these latter journals represent the mainstreaming of B&NE research while the former journals represent the development of new ideas and the development of a field separate from the mainstream?

Network mapping of the B&NE field

In our prior four volume set (Georg and Hoffman, 2013), we were asked to select 70 articles that represented the major foci of the B&NE field. We selected articles based on past impact (measured by citation count), potential future impact in the field (measured by citations per year)[3] and empirical and theoretical diversity (measured by what we saw as the scope of streams and conversations taking place). Our list (shown in Appendix II) therefore, does not include all major citations of the field. For example, while there were a great number of articles on the topic of "whether it pays to be green?" that emerged in the 1990s and had a great influence on the development of the field, we chose only a small number of that stream in order to make room for a more representative scope of papers to depict the field. Figure 2.3 presents the citation network among these works based in Histcite© mapping software.[4] Several observations become immediately apparent in this map.

First, there are 11 highly cited articles that are central to the map. These articles include article 2 (Wood, 1991), 10 (Gladwin, Kennelly and Krause, 1995), 11 (Starik and Rands, 1995), 12 (Shrivastava, 1995a), 13 (Hart, 1995), 14 (Jennings and Zandbergen, 1995), 17 (Hart, 1997), 19 (Russo and Fouts, 1997), 20 (Mitchell, Agle and Wood, 1997), 23 (Sharma and Vredenburg, 1998) and 26 (Hoffman, 1999).

Second, these articles are highly concentrated in the mid-1990s with five of the 11 appearing in a 1995 special issue of *Academy of Management Review*, while the other highly cited articles appear in other top journals, notably *Academy of Management Journal* and *Strategic Management Journal*. The topics addressed in these articles include the strategic implications of environmental concerns and the development of theoretical frameworks to address the issues of B&NE, notably institutional theory, resource-based view of the firm and stakeholder theory.

Third, articles 1 (Hahn and Stavins, 1991), 3 (Gray, 1992), 4 (Wood, 1991), 6 (Thierry et al., 1995), 8 (Wapner, 1995), 25 (Georg, 1999), 32 (Klassen and Whybark, 1999), 34 (King and Lenox, 2001a), 40 (Sarkis, 2003), 59 (MacKenzie, 2009), 60 (Nidumolu, Prahalad and Rangaswami,

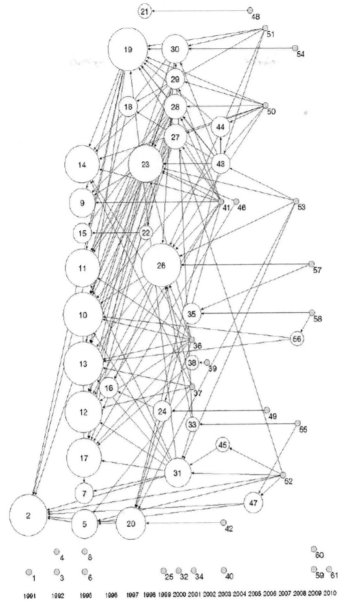

Figure 2.3 Histcite© network map of B&NE articles, 1991–2010 (see Appendix II for article codes)

2009) and 61 (Shove and Walker, 2010) are completely separate from the network map. Moreover, these contributions come from fields separate from the more mainstream B&NE fields of organizational theory and strategy: 1 (economics), 3 (accounting), 4 (European management), 6 (operations), 8 (political science), 25 (ecological economics), 32 (operations), 34 (though this is a strategy paper, it appears in an operations journal), 40 (operations), 59 (accounting), 60 (Base of the Pyramid) and 61 (political science).

Fourth, most of the operations papers in the sample do not cite each other or those in the broader network. Article 49 (Vachon and Klassen, 2006) is an operations paper that is integrated into the network but with only one tie to article 24 (Henriques and Sadorsky, 1999). Article 38 (Corbett and Kirsch, 2001) is in an operations journal but about industry standards with only two ties (to articles 39 [Delmas, 2002] and 17 [Hart, 1997]).

Fifth, there is a distinctly European conversation taking place on the role of technology in ensuring societal transitions (see articles 2, Kemp, Schot and Hoogma, 1998, and 48, Smith, Stirling and Berkhout, 2005). And, there is a semi-distinct conversation that centers on Corporate Social Responsibility (CSR), with a bridge to a broader conversation on the role of stakeholders, among articles 2 (Wood, 1991), 5 (Clarkson, 1995), 20 (Mitchell, Agle, and Wood, 1997), 45 (Bansal and Clelland, 2004), 47 (Matten and Crane, 2005) and 52 (Aguilera et al., 2007), and linking with 31 (Bansal and Roth, 2000). This represents a significant stream of research that forms a foundational element of B&NE research.

Sixth, the picture of the B&NE field depicted in figure 2.3 indicates a multifaceted landscape of the research discourse and returns us to an important question for B&NE scholars: Is there one concise and intact field called B&NE, or does it represent a composite of relatively specialized (and even disconnected) streams of research? While figure 2.3 illustrates that there is a core body of literature that is commonly referenced (indicated by the large nodes), some articles (and authors) appear to be talking more to each other than to the broader field. This could be an artifact of our sample selection, but it is a broader question that many within the field have been asking as they seek to provoke conversation among multiple disciplinary approaches.

Seventh and finally, the depiction of the field shown in figure 2.3 raises questions about the geographic representation at the field's academic core. Our choice of articles has a strong US focus: of the 61 texts included in figure 2.3 approximately two-thirds of them are authored by scholars affiliated with US universities and a handful are co-authored by Canadian and US scholars, while the remaining articles have been written by scholars from affiliated universities in other countries, notably the United Kingdom. This mirrors a citation pattern found within organizational theory in general: the field is dominated by work from North America, predominantly the United States (March, 2007). Moreover, if one considers who quotes whom, it is clear that North American authors are cited more heavily in the work of non-North Americans than vice versa. In our sample it looks as if North Americans primarily cite North Americans. Although this may, perhaps, be attributed to a bias in our material, others have observed this pattern as well (Meyer and Boxenbaum, 2010). With so few of the authors being from non-English speaking countries (i.e. Spain, the Netherlands and Denmark), it is fair to say that the dominant language in B&NE research is English.

The B&NE field matures

Beginning in 2010, attention to B&NE topics within the management literature begins to reach a plateau. Though articles with the keyword of sustainability eclipsed those with natural environment as a keyword by a ratio of over 7 to 1 (roughly 275,000 to 35,000), both seem to have reached a stall in growth. Shown in figure 2.4, articles with the keywords "business" and "natural environment" (as found in Googlescholar©) reached a peak of roughly 40,000/year between 2010 and 2012. Figure 2.5 shows a similar trend for articles with the keywords "business" and "sustainability" (as found in googlescholar©) though the peak is much higher. And as shown in figure 2.6, these trends match trends in membership in the Organizations & Natural Environment Division of the Academy of Management, which plateaued in 2010. This evolution of keywords could offer clues as the decline of articles in both categories between 2010 and 2016. For example, new keywords with greater specificity (such as circular economy, sharing economy, human rights, living wages, human trafficking, etc.) are possibly supplanting the more encompassing B&NE or business sustainability as the field further develops. Regardless, this maturing of the field is a natural expression of the lifespan of any domain of inquiry, emerging as a new idea and developing as a growing body of literature until it reaches some stable level in which its scholars can begin to dig more deeply into its underlying elements (Downs, 1972).

In sum, this chapter has offered a statistical analysis of a large corpus of B&NE research. It provides a useful snapshot for assessing the overall landscape of the field. In the next chapter, we offer a layout of the field by providing an overview of its key themes and critical domains of inquiry.

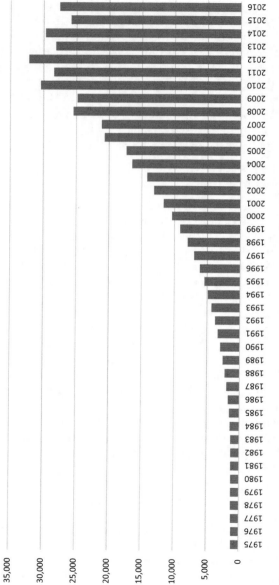

Figure 2.4 Academic articles using the keywords "business" and "natural environment" on Google Scholar, 1975–2017 (five-year rolling averages)

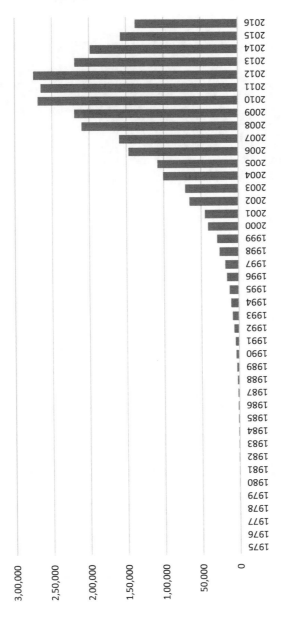

Figure 2.5 Academic articles using the keywords "business" and "sustainability" on Google Scholar, 1975–2017 (five-year rolling averages)

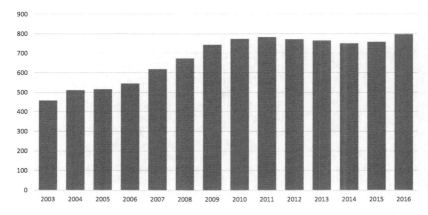

Figure 2.6 Membership in the Organizations & Natural Environment Division of the Academy of Management, 2003–2016

Notes

1 This list of articles was created by merging the bibliographies of the 38 chapters published in *The Oxford Handbook of Business and the Natural Environment* (Bansal and Hoffman, 2012). The chapters, written by 65 B&NE scholars representing 10 countries and three continents, cover each of the disciplines found in a business school – strategy, business policy, organizational theory, operations, marketing, accounting and finance, as well as sections for emergent and future perspectives. Authors were asked to write from their particular discipline and discuss where the field has been, is now and will be in the future on the topic of B&NE. Authors were also asked to make their bibliographies as inclusive as possible of what might be considered the seminal papers of the field in their particular discipline. The merged bibliographies created a total of 874 articles which represent a database proxy of the B&NE field as defined by 65 scholars of the field. One observation of this list is that there are far more North American articles than European. This may be due to the combined effect of journal rankings and the imperative for scholars on both sides of the Atlantic to publish in highly ranked journals, which predominantly are North American journals.
2 These citation counts were recorded in 2012.
3 Were we to create a ratio of citations per year to overall citation count in Appendix II, those articles that rank higher on the list for citations per year than overall citation count may be considered to be up and coming articles relative to their peer set (presuming their citation trend continues). Those articles with a higher citation count rank than citations per year rank may be considered to be sun setting in influence relative to their peer set.
4 Histcite© uses the Web of Science© database to create citations maps. Nine articles in our sample are not listed in Web of Science© because they are either too old, they are book chapters or they are in journals that are not cited in the database. The key code for the articles can be found in Appendix II. The size of the circle indicates the number of overall citations, and the arrows refer to who cites who. The size of the circles for the more recent articles are expected to be smaller, given the reduced amount of time in which the articles can be cited.

3 The field matures

Multiple conversations that comprise the B&NE field

Any attempt to structure and characterize a research domain is certain to be contentious. There will be many that will disagree with our choices, both for what we have included and what we have left out. Again, we do not propose to be the definitive final word on institutionalizing the field. But, in our attempt at such a task, we hope to stimulate conversation among B&NE scholars to come to greater clarity over who we are and where we are going. In conceptualizing the multiple conversations that comprise the B&NE field, we offer three categories: (1) conceptual models for considering environmental issues within the management literature, (2) considerations for the drivers of corporate environmental action and (3) organizational responses to such pressures. This list can serve as a map or guide for new and junior scholars to consider how to enter and contribute to a field with many sub-specializations.

Conceptual models

Much early B&NE research sought to establish a new paradigm on its own, one that did not draw from existing literatures in mainstream business. However, this began to change in the mid-1990s as noted in a call from Gladwin (1993) to clarify "The meaning of greening." Not only did this paper issue a "plea" for using organizational theory in analyzing how businesses grapple with environmental issues, it also criticized B&NE research for being too ideologically informed, lacking in precise definitions, providing low-quality empirical findings and not being cumulative or building upon previous work (Gladwin, 1993). With that call, B&NE research began to anchor on existing debates within other disciplines, most notably environmental philosophy, sociology and economics. And, in the ensuing years, the field branched out to engage with rigorous application of multiple theoretical lenses, most predominantly in the disciplines of strategy and organizational theory.

This section will overview early discussions of five mainstream conceptual models – the economics of linking environmental and financial performance, competitive strategy, resource-based view, institutional theory and stakeholder theory. Although there is a continued interest in economic consequences of addressing environmental problems, fewer studies appear to be informed by the resource-based view than by institutional and/or stakeholder theory. This section also highlights research from two domains in which the field still seeks to defy mainstream theorizing attempts: one which places more emphasis on natural ecology and the other is work based on critical theory.

Linking environmental and financial performance

Within B&NE research, the relationship between business success and environmental protection has been subject of much attention. A one-page commentary on the conflict between environmental protection and economic competitiveness in *Scientific American* (Porter, 1991) challenged conventional economic wisdom regarding this relationship and set a new stream in motion. Prior to that paper, the interests of economic growth and environmental protection had been treated primarily in oppositional, zero-sum terms. Investments in environmental protection were considered unproductive and, therefore, likely to undermine corporate competitiveness. Instead, Porter (1991) argued that this was a false dichotomy based on a static view of competition. Drawing upon the paradigm of dynamic competitiveness developed in the 1980s, he argued that environmental concerns could, if regulations were sufficiently stringent, be turned into a competitive advantage.

This essay led to a great deal of coverage of the question of whether it "pays to be green" in both the scholarly and popular literature. Initially formed as a debate among economists and strategy scholars (Porter and van der Linde, 1995; Walley and Whitehead, 1994), it grew to encompass researchers from other disciplines (Barnett and Salomon, 2006; Boon and Wagner, 2009; King and Lenox, 2001a; Waddock and Graves, 1997; Wood, 1991). And yet, despite well-developed theoretical arguments and numerous studies, the answer to this question continues to be uncertain (Margolis and Walsh, 2003; Orlitzky, Schmidt and Rynes, 2003). Many researchers have therefore suggested that the question needs to be reformulated. Instead of asking "if" it pays to be green, attention should refocus on "how" and "when" it pays to be green (Howard-Grenville and Hoffman, 2003; King and Lenox, 2001a; Margolis and Walsh, 2003; Siegel, 2009).

Today, nearly 30 years later, the question of whether it pays to be green continues to be unresolved (Hoffman and Bansal, 2012: 14). There are, according to Edrikat et al. (2014), several reasons for why this is the case: much of the research lacks a clear theoretical grounding or clear idea of the direction of causality; there are inconsistencies in defining and measuring the constructs of interest because of their multidimensionality; and many of the models are misspecified. Nevertheless, Edrikat et al.'s meta-analytical review of the literature (2014), suggests that the relationship between corporate environmental and financial performance is generally positive, and it is stronger for more proactive approaches to improving environmental performance.

Competitive strategy

Beyond this central strand of discourse, there are two streams within the strategy literature that have drawn significant attention. The older of the two begins with discussion of a shifting paradigm, out of which could emerge new environmental strategies (Gladwin, Kennelly and Krause, 1995); the second is the redefinition of generic strategies, addressing how low-cost, differentiation and niche strategies of firms can influence environmental performance (Reinhardt, 1998; Shrivastava, 1995a). Also in this vein are a number of studies characterizing corporate environmental strategies as ranging from reactive regulatory compliance to proactive corporate behavior (Hunt and Auster, 1990; Post and Altman, 1992; Schmidheiny, 1992) and offering analysis of the determinants of environmental performance (Christmann, 2000; Henriques and Sadorsky, 1996). While much of this research has been conducted during times of relative economic prosperity, more recent research on corporate strategy during times of economic distress – recession – indicate that firms both trim and focus their sustainability programs (i.e. seek to extract more value from existing sustainability activities) while also focusing on the more strategic of these activities at the expense of more tactical initiatives (Barnett et al., 2015).

Resource-based view

One characteristic feature and output of much of the early work on competitive strategy was to direct attention into the processes that take place within the "black box" of a firm to drive it to be "green." One of the central domains for this inquiry is the resource-based view of the firm, and its variant, the natural resource based view (Hart, 1995). This strand of the corporate strategy literature focused on the ways in which corporate environmental strategies are implemented, and, importantly, how those strategies are configured based on developments in the external environment. In a sense this perspective offered an "outside-in" view of competitive advantage. But with an emphasis on the internal competencies of the firm, it blended this perspective with an "inside-out" view. Competitive advantage was seen as rooted in how a firm links its core competencies to resources in the firm's external environment. This perspective directs attention to organizational capabilities to leverage key resources.

But going further, Hart (1995: 986) criticized the resource-based view for one glaring and serious omission: "It systematically ignores the constraints imposed by the biophysical (natural) environment," which, in his view, rendered the theory incomplete. As an alternative, Hart (1995) suggested a "natural-resource-based view" where a firm's competitive advantage was seen as rooted in its capabilities to undertake activities that are environmentally sustainable. To this end, Hart argued that there were three stages of proactive environmental strategy, each involving strategic capabilities – pollution prevention, product stewardship and sustainable development – which differ in terms of external driving forces, necessary resources and source of competitive advantage.

With this critical addition, the resource based view has been put to widespread use in numerous analyzes of corporate environmental strategy (Aragón-Correa and Sharma, 2003; Russo and Fouts, 1997; Shrivastava, 1995a). This stream of research paid particular attention to the development of competitively valuable organizational capabilities (Hart, 1995; Sharma and Vredenberg, 1998), absorptive capacity (Delmas, Hoffmann and Kuss, 2011; Lenox and King, 2004) and complementary assets (Christmann, 2000) as key levers for creating competitive advantage through environmental performance. These studies acknowledged that external stakeholders provide an important impetus for change that can improve organizational performance, thus adding to the growing understanding of how the external environment can influence the development of corporate environmental strategies and valuable organizational capabilities (Aragón-Correa and Sharma, 2003; Sharma and Vredenburg, 1998). Further, this work introduced notions of uncertainty, complexity and munificence to a firm's external environment, which can moderate the competitive value of proactive environmental strategies. In this way, the resource based view offered explanations of why firms with similar resources may perform differently by either developing different environmental strategies and/or obtaining different economic results while relying on similar environmental strategies.

This work has primarily focused on analyzing pollution prevention strategies, and paid less attention to the development and competitive impact of product stewardship and sustainable development strategies (Hart and Dowell, 2011). The latter is thought of in terms of clean technology strategies and "Base of the Pyramid" strategies (Hart, 1997; 2007; London,

2016; Prahalad and Hart, 2002), both of which were heralded as a means for enabling "green" or "sustainable growth." In light of the growing economic, environmental and social challenges facing business and society, the original argument for recasting the resource-based view of the firm has, according to Hart and Dowell (2011: 1476), "only become stronger and more relevant."

Institutional theory

Inherent in much of the strategy literature on corporate environmentalism is an efficiency argument: sustained competitive advantage depends on the firms' strategic choices or the leveraging of its' capabilities, resources and assets (Hart, 1995; Porter and van der Linde, 1995). However, viewed through the lens of institutional theory, other factors need to be considered. Firms also have to behave in ways that are considered "legitimate" by powerful social actors within their institutional environments.

In the often-cited special issue of *Academy of Management Review*, Jennings and Zandbergen (1995) were among the first to demonstrate the usefulness of institutional theory in analyzing corporate environmental behavior. They pointed to the processes through which the institutionalization of ecological concerns can take place and to how these processes could influence what "organizational sustainability" might mean. Although the notion of organizational sustainability has since been subject to critique (Banerjee, 2003; 2008; Sterman, 2012; Roome, 2012), Jennings and Zandbergen were one of the early works in what has become a solid stream of B&NE research.

In another early paper, Hoffman (1999) built a framework for understanding the co-evolution of organizational fields, institutions and organizational structure. He theorized organizational fields as forming around key issues – in this case environmental protection – and considered them as arenas for debate, contestation and interpretation. Hoffman demonstrated that corporate environmental strategy is shaped by the field, and not just as a matter of strategic choice, thus, qualifying claims that economic and environmental performance automatically go hand-in-hand.

A central implication of firm behavior being shaped by constituents in the field is that of organizational and institutional isomorphism: as more and more organizations conform with "rationalized myths" as to what is the proper course of action, they come to resemble one another more and the myths become more entrenched or institutionalized. The diffusion of organizational ideas and practices is the key mechanism, and it takes place through the regulatory, normative and/or cognitive pressures that firms face. With this as an orienting structure, B&NE studies focused on how environmental regulation, as a coercive force, has influenced firms to develop clean technologies (Ashford, 1993; Ashford, Ayres and Stone, 1985; Georg, 1994; Kemp, 1993), environmental management systems (Henriques and Sadorsky, 1996) and environmental strategies (Aragon-Corres, 1998; Nehrt, 1998).

In light of the growth of environmental regulation from the 1970s onward, this interest in the regulatory "drivers" is hardly surprising. But with the advent of voluntary approaches and an increase in industry self-regulation in the 1990s and 2000s, the number of studies that focused on normative influences increased, as witnessed by the many studies of industry associations and certification agencies that influence the diffusion of environmental management systems such as ISO 14001 and the European counterpart, EMAS (Bansal and Roth, 2000; Delmas, 2002; King and Lenox, 2000; King, Lenox and Terlaak, 2005). While both the regulatory and normative pressures for environmental change have received quite a bit of attention, cognitive pressures have received comparatively less attention. One of the reasons for this gap is that they are more difficult to identify and isolate empirically; and are at best captured by proxies such as discourse. Also, the three types of pressures are more difficult to disentangle empirically than theoretically.

Although there has been and still is much interest in how widely accepted ideas and practices diffuse across industries, there is a growing interest in explaining why companies within the same field respond differently (Lounsbury, 2001). One stream of this research draws attention to the importance of social movements and occupational groups as inter- and intra-organizational linkages that can filter inputs from the field to the organization (Hoffman, 2001b). Corporate environmentalism in this view is theorized as the result of institutional pressures as well as the organizational structure, communication patterns and culture. Delmas and Toffel (2008) have demonstrated the empirical relevance of Hoffman's (1999, 2001a) model in their study of how institutional pressures are channeled to different organizational functions and how this influences the ways in which these signals are received.

A second stream of institutional research focused on the ability of firms to defy institutional pressures by acting as "institutional entrepreneurs" (DiMaggio, 1988; Fligstein, 1997; Lawrence, 1999) in shaping the discourse, norms and the structures that guide organizational action (Maguire, Hardy and Lawrence, 2004). This research focused on change as the outcome of concerted and organized action. But strategic deviance can also take the form of stasis, as firms conform symbolically to institutional pressures by decoupling their core activities from the practices and procedures forced upon them from the outside, what is labeled as "greenwashing" (Greer and

Bruno, 1996; Lyon and Maxwell, 2011). Signaling in this way that they are doing the "right thing," the aim is to placate company stakeholders by creating a green ceremonial façade (Jermier and Forbes, 2003).

A third stream of institutional research drew from the Scandinavian approach to institutionalism (Bergström and Dobers, 2000; Boons and Strannegård, 2000; Czarniawska and Sevón, 1996). Informed by Cyert and March (1992), March (1991), Latour (1987, 1998) and Weick (1995), this approach challenged both the isomorphism and de-coupling arguments. Instead of focusing on the field and/or the institutional pressures, Scandinavian institutionalism focuses on organizational practices, and argues that practices are "translated" every time they are applied in a new context and in this way, processes are changed. This makes it difficult to assess just exactly what is being diffused (Bergström and Dobers, 2000).

More recent research has focused on examining the applicability of institutional theory to an examination of the nature of fields and how they change, particularly in the wake of trigger events that can be framed for change or for stasis (Hoffman and Jennings, 2011). As the issue of climate change manifests itself in more frequent and more severe weather events (i.e. hurricanes, droughts, wildfires and floods), the social discourse and ultimate framing of these events becomes critically important for acknowledging a shift in our notions of the natural world.

Stakeholder theory

The importance of stakeholders was canonized with the publication of *Strategic Management: A Stakeholder Approach* (Freeman, 1984), which described companies as being situated within a web of relations to others who have legitimate interests – or a stake – in what the company does. Be it the neighbors, employees, investors, insurance companies, government, the press or others, stakeholders can exert pressure, provide important resources and impose costs through protest. Stakeholder management entails deliberate actions to appease stakeholder concerns while simultaneously pursuing company objectives.

In light of the many stakeholders that engage around environmental issues (including regulatory agencies, environmental activists, customers, suppliers, employees and others), it is understandable that a great deal of research attention has been given to characterizing stakeholders as internal or external and primary or secondary (Clarkson, 1995), and to developing typologies to classify them (Mitchell, Agle and Wood, 1997). According to Mitchell, Agle and Wood (1997), stakeholders should be considered in terms of their power to influence the firm as well as their legitimacy and the urgency of their claims. However, due to the limited insights and cognitive barriers managers may have (Bazerman and Hoffman, 1999; Buysse and Verbeke, 2003; Kassinis and Vafeas, 2006), defining "who and what really counts" (Mitchell, Agle and Wood, 1997) is likely to be less straightforward than depicted in the literature. Another complicating factor is that both the "stakes" and the "holders" can change rapidly and unexpectedly.

Much of the work informed by stakeholder theory focused on specific stakeholder groups and analyzed how they influence corporate environmental behavior (Buysse and Verbeke, 2003; Delmas, 2001; Sharma and Henriques, 2005). Work also sought to assess how stakeholders and stakeholder management affects corporate and environmental performance (Berman et al., 1999; Harrison, Bosse and Phillips, 2010; Kassinis and Vafeas, 2006). Analogous to the work on whether it pays to be green, the findings on whether "it pays to do good" have also been inconclusive.

More recent research has focused on examining the applicability of stakeholder theory in sustainability management (Hörisch et al., 2014), and points to three challenges in managing stakeholder relationships for sustainability that warrant further research: the strengthening of stakeholders' interests in sustainability, creating mutual interests between stakeholders and the company, and finding ways to empower stakeholders in promoting sustainability. Hörisch et al. (2014) point to the importance of education, regulation and sustainability-based value creation for the stakeholders.

Incorporating the natural environment into management

While much of the B&NE literature focused on the economic, strategic and managerial aspects of changing business behavior, it paid limited attention to what happens in the natural environment. One such formative study that began to focus explicitly on the natural environment took place in 1997 when 13 economists, ecologists and geographers conducted an analysis of 17 ecosystem services and determined a value for nature to the human economy estimated at between $16 and $54 trillion per year, with a likely figure of at least $33 trillion (Costanza et al., 1997). Many environmentalists bristled at the idea of placing an economic value on nature, but the researchers used the conclusion to highlight an important point. If one compared the figure to the $18 trillion gross national product (GNP) of the world, it became clear that the services provided by nature exceeded the services provided by the human economy. Protecting nature, they argued, should therefore be given greater importance in relation to our own economic considerations.

Coincident with this study, there were a number of strands of work seeking to forge stronger links between what happens to the natural environment and the social activities taking place in and around companies (Costanza et al., 1997; Crane, Matten and Moon, 2008; Egri and Pinfield, 1996; Starik and Rands, 1995). On a general note, and inspired by the debate about the dominant economic paradigm versus a new ecological paradigm (Catton and Dunlap, 1980), there were calls for a reconceptualization of the organizational environment and a stronger integration between the natural environment and organizational perspectives (Bansal and Roth, 2000; Egri and Pinfield, 1996). This stream pointed to the need for developing eco-centric approaches to business management and recognized that there are limits to growth under existing models (Gladwin, Kennelly and Krause, 1995; Meadows et al., 1972). This critique has been taken a bit further in a broadside critique of capitalism and a call for B&NE research to develop more critical and normative analyses (Gladwin, 2012).

There are, however, some contributions seeking to "re-work" established theories, like stakeholder theory, to bring them into line with environmental realities. Starik (1995), for example, made a case for considering the natural environment – all its living and non-living components – as stakeholders. Crane, Matten and Moon (2008) introduced the notion of ecological citizenship as a means to capture the political dimensions of corporate environmentalism. Others draw on systems thinking to capture the complexity of corporate environmentalism, where business is considered as embedded in myriads of relations, and changes in business behavior are conditioned by multiple feedback loops, time delays and unexpected effects (Egri and Pinfield, 1996; Sterman, 2012; Roome, 2012). Viewed from this perspective, the notion of a single company being sustainable has an oxymoronic ring to it.

The systemic aspects of sustainability are also associated with the Gaia hypothesis, which evolved in the beginning of the 1970s (within atmospheric chemistry) as a speculative claim about "a biological cybernetic system able to homeostat the planet for an optimum physical and chemical state appropriate to its current biosphere" (Lovelock, 1972: 579). Over the next two decades it was elaborated into a geobiological worldview that has been picked up within a variety of fields, notably those dedicated to systems thinking (Clark, 2017). Gaia figures – albeit in different ways – in the recent writings of social scientists such as Stengers (2015) and Latour (2013). Both invoke the Gaia hypothesis to warn what is at stake if the issue of climate change is not more radically addressed. For Stengers (2015), climate change is inherently linked to globalization under capitalism and the persistent and irresponsible pursual of economic growth. Latour (2013) mobilizes Gaia to underline that there are limits to what the environment can stand, and emphasizes the need for action. According to Latour, in facing the challenges of climate change:

No immunology is possible, without high sensitivity to those multiple, controversial, entangled loops. Those who are not 'quick to detect or respond to slight changes' are doomed. And those who, for some reason, interrupt, erase, background, diminish, weaken, deny, obscure, underfund, or disconnect any of those loops are not only insensitive and unresponsive – they are simply criminal.

(Latour, 2013: 96, in Clark, 2017: 23)

Latour contributed to the development of political ecology by arguing that, considering the complex entanglements between "the social" and "the natural environment," nature is not "pure" or untouched by humans and in need of protection (Latour, 1998). With its emphasis on the interrelationships between socio-political and economic factors and environmental issues, political ecology has clear bearing for the analysis of B&NE.

Critical theory

When considering the theories most commonly evoked in the B&NE literature, one can conclude that the apple does not fall far from the tree, given that the theoretical grounding of much of the literature is within the mainstream of organizational and management theory. Although hardly surprising, if one considers the development of a field in terms of extending extant theories to new empirical domains, many are, nevertheless, critical of the way in which B&NE research has developed (Banerjee, 2008; 2012; Gladwin, 2012). Some argue that the field has been "hijacked" (Welford, 1997); that it should have a stronger eco-centric focus (Egri and Pinfield, 1996); that it should look beyond the needs of Northern elites (Gladwin, Newburry, and Reiskin, 1997); that it pays too little attention to the power and politics at play (Latour, 1998; Orsato and Clegg, 2002; Orsato, den Hond and Clegg, 1999; Springett, 2003); and is, by and large, separated and oblivious to the environmental harms that continue to escalate in the natural world (Gladwin, 2012). This may be attributed to B&NE research's emphasis on business success rather than natural environment stability, but it could also be that mainstream theories are "blind" to certain issues and that we need to develop different lenses through which we can view and assess the relationship between business and the natural environment. In what follows, we point to two such lenses, critical management studies and actor-network theory.

Authors in critical management studies focus on the power, politics and forms of resistance involved in developing corporate sustainability and ensuring sustainable development (Banerjee, 2008; Levy, 1997; Orsato and Clegg, 1999). Rather than assuming that these terms can be easily defined or that they are unproblematic, critical approaches attend to the discursive, material, institutional power plays that confer legitimacy to the ways in which business deals with environmental issues and offers skeptical accounts of business behavior, particularly with regard to how it impacts the lives of more impoverished and marginal stakeholders (Banerjee, 2008).

Authors drawing upon actor network theory, within the realm of Science and Technology Studies, offer another critical lens for analyzing the interrelations between business and the natural environment (Callon, 1986; Latour, 1987; Law, 1992). This literature addresses some of the same overarching research questions as institutional theory and critical management studies (i.e. understanding how certain practices become institutionalized and the power play involved) but it is premised on an assumption that both human and non-human actors must both be considered when explaining how relations arise and are changed. Actor network theory seeks to capture both the material and symbolic aspects of change processes (Czarniawska, 2009) and scholars informed by this approach argue that the relationship between business and the natural environment is an effect and an outcome of the complex entanglements between human and non-human actors through which their possibilities to act are negotiated, transformed and translated (Newton, 2002; Newton and Harte, 1997). Rather than making claims as to the merits or drawbacks of corporate environmentalism (and/or CSR), emphasis is given to how these concepts unfold in practice (Bergström and Diedrich, 2011; Bergström and Dobers, 2000). In other words, it is concerned with how they are enacted. From this perspective, it is important to pay attention to the mundane materials and practices that go into making corporate environmental performance, and in this way actor network theory lends itself to the gerundial shift within organizational theory (Weick, 1979) to studying organiz*ing* rather than formal organizations.

Contributions from both critical theory and actor network theory have recently been extended to studies of climate policy and the intricacies of what it takes to create a market for carbon (Callon, 2009; MacKenzie, 2009). Based on the idea that "economics does not describe an existing external 'economy', but brings that economy into being: economics performs the economy, creating the phenomena it describes" (MacKenzie and Millo, 2003: 108), these studies document how greenhouse gas emissions permits are framed through economic calculations and become objects that can be bought and sold on the (CO_2) market. Although one can contend that the making of a carbon market is a political project aimed as internalizing pollution costs (externalities), they argue that political decisions are not enough and that formal technical definitions are necessary to clarify which kinds of greenhouse gases have to be made commensurable and made visible in economic terms (MacKenzie, 2009: 447). This perspective points to the important role of professional understandings and instruments needed to make something knowable, valuable and actionable.

Disparate as these theoretically informed conversations may be, they each point to limitations in the mainstream B&NE research. But equally, if not more importantly, they also ask questions that the mainstream B&NE literature does not. Each of these perspectives extends analysis beyond the interests of a single firm or organization and emphasizes the contentiousness in bringing about deep transformative environmental change. By asking us to consider the fundamental structures, the values of our current modes of organizing and how these values are created, they present new and provocative understandings and routes for research, and thus, extend the field in new directions.

Drivers of change

The question of what drives business companies to improve their environmental performance is, not surprisingly, a recurring question in B&NE research's many guises. Even though there may be almost any number of factors influencing firm behavior, this section focuses on the four drivers that figure prominently in the literature – government regulation, industry self-regulation, consumer pressure and social movements. The order in which these drivers are listed is also indicative of shifts in our understanding of who can bring about environmental change and the politics by which this happens. What was once the sole domain of government has, over time, given rise to new areas of inquiry that encompass other modes of governance.

Government regulation

Environmental regulation was introduced in most (Western) industrialized countries at more or less the same time in the 1970s, and these countries have continued to add to these regulatory frameworks ever since. In light of these developments, it is not surprising that there is a large body of B&NE research dedicated to examining effect of this regulation on, notably, the economic performance of companies (Barnett and Salomon, 2006; King and Lenox, 2001a; Waddock and Graves, 1997), the development of clean technology (Kemp, 1993; Schot, 1992), innovation (Ashford, 1993; OECD, 2000) and the introduction of environmental management systems (Dahlmann and Brammer, 2011; Delmas, 2001; Khanna and Anton, 2002). Although some have argued that regulatory policies will work differently depending on industry and company characteristics (i.e. some policies will evoke proactive behavior in some industries/companies and not in others) (Dahlmann and Brammer, 2011; Hunt and Auster, 1990), it appears that even within the same industries there are substantial differences in regulatory response (Prakash and Kellman, 2004). These differences may be attributed to, for instance, differences in managerial perceptions, strategic action, organizational culture, operational imperatives or institutional environments.

For example, a study of US firms participating in the US Dept. of Energy's Climate Challenge Program (1995–2000), a voluntary agreement with electrical utilities to reduce greenhouse gas emissions, showed that there were substantial differences in the strategies pursued by firms, depending on when they entered the voluntary agreement (Delmas and Montes-Sancho, 2010). Late joiners were more likely to pursue symbolic cooperation whereas early joiners had more substantive cooperative strategies. The differences in these responses is attributed to differences in institutional pressures.

While much of the early research focused on the "dirtiest" industries (i.e. the extraction, oil, chemical and manufacturing industries) (Jänicke, Binder and Mönch, 1997; Sharma and Henriques, 2005) and on the use of mandatory regulations regarding specific environmental targets and/or emission standards, attention eventually shifted both to other industries (i.e. electronics, information technology and tourism) and other regulatory instruments and environmental policy goals. For example, there has been a marked increase in research on the use of voluntary negotiated agreements and market-based instruments such as environmental taxes, and emission trading schemes. The introduction of voluntary negotiated agreements does not imply abandoning the use of mandatory measures. Quite the contrary, in many instances the use of negotiated voluntary agreements is supported by credible threats of a mandatory approach, should the voluntary scheme fail (Georg, 1994; Labatt and Maclaren, 1998; Potoski and Prakash, 2004). The use of negotiated voluntary agreements is, however, more common in Europe than in the United States (Glachant, 1994; OECD, 2003).

Research on market-based instruments has been founded on conventional analyses that consider the economic efficiency of such instruments over "command and control" regulation (Hahn and Stavins, 1991). For example, although the introduction of market-based instruments led to the reduction of sulfur dioxide emissions in the US, the failure of negotiations to institute a carbon trading scheme that works (Carter, Clegg, and Wåhlin, 2011; MacKenzie, 2009) calls the effectiveness and broad applicability of these instruments into question. This prompts a need for further empirical analysis of, for example, the benefits some industries derive from influencing and lobbying regulators to introduce regulatory measures that fit their needs (Perrow, 2010; Reinhardt, 1998; 1999; Vogel, 2005).

Industry self-regulation

Industry self-regulation is an umbrella term for the myriad of activities that industry, notably industry associations, introduce to regulate corporate behavior and competition (i.e. certification schemes such as the ISO14000 series or its European counterpart, EMAS) (Corbett and Kirsch, 2001; Darnall and Sides, 2008; Delmas, 2002). There are two forces driving the introduction of self-regulatory systems – the problems of asymmetric information and market failure (Barnett and King, 2008; King and Lenox, 2000). In the first instance, self-regulated information disclosure can be a means to reduce asymmetries and gain positive reputational benefits. In the second instance, self-regulated compliance programs can entail the development of a collective defense mechanism that can either help forestall and preempt government regulation, or "weed out" poor environmental performers so as to minimize the detrimental reputational effect of the industry as a whole with regulators.

Much of the research on industrial self-regulation focuses on the economic and environmental performance of companies as compared to the absence of such a program, or the implementation of formal regulatory measures (King, Lenox and Terlaak, 2005; Terlaak and King, 2006; Toffel, 2006). Other studies consider the reasons why certification has become so widespread (Delmas, 2002; Delmas and Toffel, 2004), whether self-regulatory actions have the desired effect on recalcitrant companies within the industry (King and Lenox, 2000; Lenox and Nash, 2003; Rivera and de Leon, 2005) and the importance of sanctions for self-regulatory actions to work (Lenox and Nash, 2003).

Much of this work shows that industrial self-regulation often falls short of desired economic and environmental ends (Barnett and King, 2008; Darnall and Sides, 2008). For example, one study of US industries (Short and Toffel, 2010) found that concurrent legal environments for effective enforcement activities of corporate compliance to self-regulatory schemes helped ensure greater success. So, while industry continues to have a strong interest in this particular governance approach, research suggests that self-regulation cannot replace conventional command and control regulation.

Consumer pressure

The role of consumers in environmental performance is an obvious one – they influence company behavior by either buying or not buying company products and services. The extent to which environmental issues are influencing the buying habits of consumers is not clear, despite commonplace references to and calls for "green consumerism." While much of the research in this area has centered on characterizing green consumers, identifying their values and assessing motivations for their choosing green products (Kilbourne and Beckmann, 1998), it is not clear how widespread a phenomenon green consumerism has become (Pedersen and Neergaard, 2006) and what effect it may be having on company performance (Eriksson, 2004) or marketing practices (Peattie, 2001).

Studies have analyzed the linkages between green products and consumer identification with a company or its strategy (Bhattacharya and Sen, 2003). Others have shown that the environmental awareness of many consumers is relatively low (Fineman and Clarke, 1996) and that they often are skeptical of company claims (Bjørner, Hansen and Russell, 2004). Other studies find that consumers have a tendency to free ride and let others, notably those in developing countries, suffer the environmental costs of consumer goods production. Research also finds that consumers have a tendency to over-discount the future (Wade-Benzoni and Tost, 2009), thereby minimizing the power of consumer behavior in addressing long-term issues like climate change and population growth. These studies highlight the mismatch between the way markets, and notably retail markets, work and the conditions that are ideal for fostering green consumerism (Gershoff and Irwin, 2012).

Much of this literature is focused on the individual end-consumer and explains consumer behavior in terms of behavioral and cognitive theory. There is, however, a growing body of literature on the greening of household consumption that draws upon (social) practice theory (Schatzki, Cetina, and von Savigny, 2001; Shove, 2003; Shove et al., 2008; Shove and Pantzar, 2005; Warde, 2005) to study issues like energy-use (Gram-Hanssen, 2010) and information and communication technologies (Røpke, Christensen, and Jensen, 2010) that attend both to the individual and contextual influences on (household) consumption.

Social movements

Tree lovers, citizens against genetically modified organisms (GMOs), anti-nuke activists and many kinds of NIMBY'ists (not-in-my-back-yard activists) have at least one thing in common – they are concerned with the ways in which production and consumption patterns are affecting the natural environment. While many of these groups are acting on the behalf of others – animals, trees, the planet and future generations – and link to broader concerns such as "the treadmill of production" (Schnaiberg, 1980) and environmental injustice and social emancipation (Banerjee, 2008), there are myriad environmental concerns driving citizens to take action in multiple organized ways (Georg, 1999). Much of this work begins with a notion that collective interests and concerns are not "given" or pre-existing, but are generally considered to be socially constructed (Coglianese, 2001; Jennings and Zandbergen, 1995; Macnaghten and Urry, 1998; Yearley, 1992). In many cases, science is used to help stake their claims and confer legitimacy to their concerns in social and political debates (Yearly, 1992).

Research on how environmentally concerned groups affect business emphasizes three approaches: (1) lobbying for changes in government regulation and polices, (i.e. NGO protests that prompted an EU moratorium on GMOs in food) (Ansell and Vogel, 2006; Doh and Guay, 2006); (2) more adversarial tactics such as the issuing of lawsuits, extensive media exposure and boycotting (King, 2008); and (3) more collaborative approaches where environmental groups work with business to develop new products or services, such as environmental groups assisting in the development of renewable energy technology markets (Sine and Lee, 2009), citizen groups collaborating with construction firms to build eco-villages (Georg and Irwin, 2002) and the creation of certification and auditing schemes to help business change behavior, notably in connection with agricultural production in developing countries (Arts, 2002). This activity takes place on multiple scales from the local to the international (Wapner, 1995). While there is a rather substantial body of literature focusing on how environmental groups can influence business, there is less research on the influence that business can have on the environmental organizations and on how the two organizations co-evolve.

Organizational response

There is a large body of research dedicated to understanding how companies respond to environmental issues, and the context in which those responses occur. In this section, we will cover four organizational domains for analyzing business response – organization and culture, framing and discourse, individual and managerial perception, and disclosure and reporting – and four broader domains in which these responses take place – multi-national corporate context, clean-tech and entrepreneurship, supply chain management and industrial ecology.

Organization and culture

One of the vexing questions in B&NE research is why firms have such varied responses to environmental issues. Although some attribute this to organizational capabilities (Aragón-Correa and Sharma, 2003; Sharma and Vredenbrug, 1998) or to field level developments (Aguilera et al., 2007; Bansal, 2003; Delmas and Toffel, 2008), many researchers seek to "open the black box" of the firm by attending to organizational culture (Forbes and Jermier, 2002; Howard-Grenville, 2006). This work addresses how organizational cultures and subcultures, and the relations between them are keys to understanding how and why firms respond differentially to environmental demands. This work emphasizes how the success of environmental initiatives is hinged on the support of senior management (Bansal, 2003; Dixon and Clifford, 2007; Ramus and Steger, 2000), the importance of environmental champions as both role models and ambassadors (Andersson and Bateman, 2000; Bansal, 2003; Markusson, 2010), and the enabling influence of environmental management systems, policies and incentive schemes that affect employee behavior (Douglas, 2007; Ramus and Steger, 2000; Smith and Brown, 2003). However, less attention has been given to how managers integrate social, environmental and economic consideration into their day-to-day management decisions and how they deal with competing demands regarding social, environmental and economic performance (Epstein et al., 2015).

Framing and discourse

The meaning given to environmental concerns is, to a large extent, dependent upon how they are framed through the discourse that constitutes these concerns as legitimate and worthy of attention. Discourse can be established within an organization as a particular way of seeing, understanding and interpreting environmental issues, thus having much in common with perspectives that consider culture as a "web of meaning" (Geertz, 1973), but they are most often associated with group processing and societal debate (Drysek, 1997; Hajer, 1997).

Research within this area focuses on how companies seek to influence environmental discourses, ranging from discourses regarding the company itself (Bansal and Clelland, 2004) to broader environmental discourse on climate change, exemplified by the heated debates between climate skeptics and large parts of the scientific communities within the natural sciences (Hoffman, 2011a; 2011b; 2015). Whilst the first-mentioned line of research addresses some of the same issues as research on company disclosure, the second issue pertains to issues of institutional change, particularly to how "language games" can help to support, re-orient or completely de-institutionalize and reconstitute existing institutions (Evans and Kay, 2008; Garud, Gehman and Karnøe, 2010; Maquire and Hardy, 2009).This research relates to work being done on the rhetorical strategies of institutional entrepreneurs (Lawrence and Philips, 2004; Suddaby and Greenwood, 2005) and the path creation that leads to new markets for clean technologies (Karnøe and Garud, 2012).

Individual and managerial perceptions

While broad cultural considerations are important for understanding environmental change, much research also attends to the individual-level processes that can be considered as the micro-foundations of organizational response (Reverdy, 2006). Corporate environmental response in B&NE literature has considered the role of individual and managerial perception, particularly how these processes inform decision-making and action, at multiple organizational levels. Some of this work draws on behavioral theory, which sees individuals as attempting to act rationally but as bounded by cognitive limitations regarding their self-interests and the interests of others, both now and in the future (Bazerman and Hoffman, 1999). Others explore the issue more inductively by attending to the ways that managerial interpretations effect company choice of environmental strategies (Banerjee, 2001; Henriques and Sadorsky, 1999; Sharma, 2000). These and other studies highlight the role of experience (Ramus and Steger, 2000; Walls and Hoffman, 2012), emotions (Fineman, 1997), individual values (Bansal, 2003), network position (Bertels, Hoffman and DeJordy, 2014) and organizational context (Sharma, 2000) in providing managers with views as to possible strategies (Egri and Herman, 2000).

In keeping with some of the research on stakeholders, some point to the importance of internal and external constituencies in shaping corporate environmental perceptions and response (Andersson and Bateman, 2000; Banerjee, 2001). Others have focused on how the scope, scale and speed of organizational response is linked to the intertwining of individual perceptions and organizational values that can lead to competing agendas, mixed motives and mixed results (Bansal, 2003; Hoffman and Ocasio, 2001). For example, a study by Epstein et al. (2015) documented the paradoxical situations of conflicting demands for managers when they favor financial performance in contexts where there is a conflict with environmental and social performance, while also publicizing ways that promote (corporate) sustainability.

Disclosure and reporting

Accounting for companies' social and environmental impacts is a growing area of practice and research, in terms of both what is reported and how it is reported. In line with the accounting truism that if something "doesn't get measured then it doesn't get managed," there is a body of research that focuses on accounting techniques, and in particular, the more technical aspects of how to account for activities not traditionally included within financial accounting, such as numerical disclosures of emission data that can be made commensurate with other emissions data so as to render this information intelligible to the presumed readers (Kolk, Levy and Pinkse, 2008) and narratives of key stakeholders (Bennett and James, 1998; Ditz, Ranganathan and Banks, 1995; Gray, Bebbington, Walters and Thomson, 1995).

While much of the accounting literature is less instrumental, more analytical, and more critical of what environmental reporting can achieve (Deegan, 2002), reporting does provide some degree of visibility regarding the issues that are important to key external constituents (i.e. government, environmental activists, employees and financial markets). As such, there has been both a move to extend reporting to include issues such as climate change impacts (i.e. through the Carbon Disclosure Project), with particular emphasis given to the link between carbon disclosures and corporate strategies (Reid and Toffel, 2009) and to link such outputs to mandatory financial statement disclosure through "integrated reporting" as the next evolution beyond stand-alone environmental or sustainability reports (Eccles and Saltzman, 2011; Gray, 1992; Gray, Kouhy, and Lavers. 1995).

Given the propensity to gear reports towards basic communications objectives, some B&NE research seeks to explore whether disclosures are seeking to provide the readers with a particular picture of firm performance that may be at variance with reality. Viewed from this perspective, environmental reporting, accounting and disclosure is considered variously as a means for increasing legitimacy by managing stakeholder impressions (Neu, Warsame and Pedwell, 1998) or as a matter of "greenwash" (Jermier and Forbes, 2003; Lyon and Maxwell, 2011). There are numerous studies of how thematic content, narrative structures and language use (Cho, Roberts and Patten, 2010) can help "veil" the firm, providing one view to the readers while shielding the inner workings from external scrutiny (Hopwood, 2009).

While much of this research examines environmental reporting from an external perspective, with emphasis on the intended effect on external stakeholders, others focus on disclosure and reporting as auto-communication that enhances employee and managerial workplace identification (Morsing, 2006) or as a productive organizational device that contributes to forming rather than just informing management decisions (Georg and Justesen, 2017; Justesen and Mourtisen, 2009). According to this performative approach, accounting is not merely a means to an end (although it can be). Rather accounting produces ends that prompt action.

So, while much of the environmental accounting research is firmly grounded on a model of accounting as information production where the environment is framed as lifeless inputs and outputs that need to be managed efficiently (Russell et al., 2017), there is a growing body of work seeking to conceptualize environmental accounting differently. Analogous to the notion that it is a "machine not a camera" (MacKenzie, 2006), accounting research that treats the domain as a locale for action is growing. For example, developments within global climate policy, particularly the creation of markets in carbon emissions, provides a vibrant arena in which the performative approach to accounting and environmental concerns are closely intertwined (Callon, 2009; Hopwood, 2009; MacKenzie, 2009).

Managing in a multi-national corporate context

The role of multi-national corporations (MNCs) in the economy is controversial in both the economic (Korten, 1995), and the environment domains (Gladwin and Welles, 1976). Historically there have been four main strands of research in this research. The first is that of "eco-imperialism" associated with MNCs through trade liberalization (Gonzalez, 2001; Paterson, Humphreys and Pettiford, 2003). The second is that of MNC "double standards" (Castleman, 1987) in which they operate with older technologies or less stringent standards of care and compensation abroad than at home. The Bhopal catastrophe is one such tragic example (Gladwin and Welles, 1976; Shrivastava, 1987). The third is the flight of MNCs to "pollution havens" in developing countries and emerging economies (Clapp, 2002; Utting, 2005). Such studies have been largely inconclusive, presumably because there are many more important factors shaping MNCs location decision than just environmental standards (Eskeland and Harrison, 2003; Javorcik and Wei, 2005).

The fourth, and most prominent area of B&NE research on MNCs, has been their positive effects in introducing uniform standards, technology transfer and the "greening" of supply chains across global operations (Christmann and Taylor, 2001). Studies of the introduction of uniform standards have focused on the difficulties of navigating among diverse institutional environments (Hunter and Bansal, 2006; Kostova, Roth and Dacin, 2008; Kostova and Zaheer, 1999), the cost reduction and efficiency gains to be made by streamlining organizational procedures (Corbett and Kirsch, 2001; Dowell, Hart and Yeung, 2000; Sharfman, Shaft and Tihanyi, 2004) and the benefits of technology transfer and growth opportunities (Hart and Milstein, 1999; Hettige et al., 1996) from the "greening" of the supply chain (Koplin, Seuring and Mesterham, 2007; Zhu and Sarkis, 2004). Much less attention is given to the negative effect that MNCs have on the environment and indigenous peoples (Banerjee, 2008), local industries (Jeppesen and Hansen, 2004) and environmental legislation nationally and internationally (Perrow, 2010).

Clean-tech and entrepreneurship

The so-called IPAT formula describing the relationship between environmental impact, population, affluence and technological development has – albeit in relatively simplistic terms – cemented the importance of technological development (Ehrlich and Ehrlich, 1991; Gladwin, 1993). As the world's population continues to grow and there is a growing demand for increased affluence, the only way in which it will be possible to minimize the overall environmental burden of these developments is through technological development. Technology is, however, often considered as having an ambivalent role when it comes to the natural environment. Some technologies are seen as being at the root of a number of environmental problems while others are considered potential "solutions," whether at the "end of pipe" or "clean(er) technologies" (Dean and McMullen, 2007; Sine, Haveman and Tolbert, 2005).

Although the market for "green" technologies is growing internationally (Jänicke and Jacob, 2004), much of the research in this area attends to the determinants on the decision to develop and/or adopt "green" technologies. Research finds that they may be strategic considerations regarding competitive advantage (Reinhardt, 1998; Shrivastava, 1995b), path dependency and the economic incentives for developing and adopting "green" technologies (Kemp and Soete, 1992; Klassen and Whybark, 1999), environmental entrepreneurship (Sine and Lee, 2009) and product recovery management (Thierry et al., 1995). Much of this work also focuses on the institutional context in which entrepreneurs and firms are embedded, and does so by mobilizing quite different theoretical domains. Some draw on institutional theory (Sine and Lee, 2009), while others draw on evolutionary economics (Geels, 2004; Kemp Schot and Hoogma, 1998; Schot, 1992), or practice theory (Shove and Walker, 2010). Others emphasize the ways in which entrepreneurs frame or qualify technologies as green, mobilize the interests of others throughout the supply chain (Sarkis, 2003; Vachon and Klassen, 2006) and enroll them in endorsing the technology (Callon, 1986; Doganova and Karnøe, 2014; Karnøe and Garud, 2012).

Supply chain management

Research in the "greening of the supply chain" has developed in the wake of industry out-sourcing to suppliers located in countries with poorer social and environmental standards. With increased media and activist scrutiny, a growing number of suppliers are being pressured to improve their environmental performance to meet purchaser requirements (Qinghua and Sarkis, 2004; Walton, Handfield and Melnyk, 1998). Research within this field focuses on three prime issue areas: (1) the strategic implications and advantages that greening the supply chain can have for companies (Corbett and De Croix, 2001; King and Lenox, 2001b; Sarkis, 2003; Vachon and Klassen, 2006; Walker, Sisto and McBain, 2008), (2) the tools that companies need in order to green their operations and assess their suppliers (Beamon, 1999; Fleischmann et al., 2001; Lenzen, 2000; Min and Galle, 1997; van Hoek, 1999; Zsidisin and Siferd, 2001), and (3) the challenges of new business opportunities associated with working with one's suppliers and with closing production loops (Bowen et al., 2001; Srivastava, 2007). These domains call for attention to both socio-economic considerations by nurturing inter-organizational relationships, developing trust (Vachon and Klassen, 2006) and technical considerations, such as through recycling and reusing of wastes or re-manufacturing these wastes into new products (Thierry et al., 1995; Geyer, van Wassenhove and Atasu, 2007).

Critics of research on sustainable supply chain management charge that it is relatively a-theoretical (Touboulic and Walker, 2015). Yet, research attention to this issue has grown substantially, particularly, in the area of the circular economy (Bocken et al., 2017; Webster, 2015). Moving away from linear models in which items are created, used and disposed of once they reach their end of serviceable life, circular models close this loop and emphasize system-wide innovation to redefine products and services in ways that their environmental performance is improved. Items are created, used and then either restored or reprocessed to recover energy or materials that can be used again. But more important, the circular economy challenges companies to design their products with the full life cycle in mind from the start, re-designing the entire production system to prioritize real social and environmental needs (versus created marketing needs), continually upcycle materials to eliminate waste and rethink the role of business in "designing for abundance" not just reducing unsustainability.

Industrial ecology

The beginning of industrial ecology as a research field is often associated with the publication of a seminal 1989 article by Frosch and Gallopolous, which posits an analogy between industrial ecosystems and biological ecosystems. This area of B&NE research is grounded on a systemic understanding of what firms can do to improve their environmental performance (Boons and Wagner, 2009; Whiteman and Cooper, 2000). Rather than focus on individual firms, this research attends to how resource use can be optimized within systems of firms (Ehrenfeld and Gertler, 1997; Erkman, 1997; Frosch and Gallopouos; 1989). Research within this domain seeks to identify and quantify the material and energy flows within and across industries, supply chains and cities (Ahi and Searcy, 2013; Lewandowski, 2016; McDonough and Braungart, 2013). Although there is a strong emphasis on the more technical aspects of measuring and analyzing these flows and on increasing resource efficiency by closing loops (Ayres, 1997; Wernick and Ausubel; 1995), there is a considerable amount of research that examines how regional industrial eco-systems work, notably the exemplar cases in the Danish town Kalundborg (Chertow, 2007; Ehrenfeld and Gertler, 1997; Jacobsen, 2006) and other parts of the world (Baas and Boons, 2007; Zhu et al., 2007).

Another key area of this research deals with the organizational aspects of industrial ecology, such as the strategic interests of those involved and the coordination, collaboration and governance issues necessary to align those interests (Boons and Baas, 1997; Esty and Porter, 1998; Lifset, 2008). Other topics addressed within the field include how life-cycle analysis, life-cycle management and life-cycle costing can be used to promote resource efficiency, and the use of reverse and forward logistics to improve operations management. Hitherto, the main thrust of this research emphasis has been on how to change production patterns, but there is a budding interest for changing consumption patterns as well (Hertwich, 2005).

The lay of the land in B&NE research?

As this chapter shows, there is a wide landscape of research within the B&NE field. The diversity of topics, empirical areas and theoretical frameworks denote a vibrant research landscape that examines the B&NE topic from a multitude of angles. Although there is a detected waning of interest in strictly business and the natural environment topics (as evidenced by a drop in research papers labeled with those topics, as shown in figures 2.4 and 2.5), there is a strong interest in the further development of some of the sub-level issues that comprise the field, such as circular economy, disclosure and reporting, supply chain management and many others. Theoretically focused work, as in institutional and stakeholder theory, continues its development and these conceptual models are being put to widespread use in a number of empirical domains pertaining to corporate social and environmental performance. As the B&NE field has evolved, issues of theoretical and conceptual grounding as well as methods used have come to figure more prominently, which is a development that mirrors that in organization and management research more generally. In the next chapter, we will assess the directions in which this B&NE research domain may be going.

4　Looking to the future of B&NE research

The future of B&NE research is moving in two directions. The first direction continues the existing streams and expands upon the foundation of research and theories that have been developed over the past two decades. The second direction represents a departure from those streams, challenging their underlying assumptions in recognition of the unprecedented environmental challenges being faced today (such as climate change) and the relative inability of existing models to address them. The marker that denotes the shift between these two streams is the emergence of the concept of the Anthropocene.

B&NE research in the era of environmental management

The roots of B&NE research lie in problem conceptions based on discrete media based concerns such as air pollution, water pollution, energy use and waste management. Solutions, therefore, have focused on approaches such as waste minimization, energy efficiency, pollution control and environmental management. In each case, the general focus of B&NE research has been to merge these existing environmental concerns with considerations for economic competitiveness and the corporate goal of gaining market advantage by making "the business case" for action (Roome, 1998; Russo and Minto, 2012; Sexton et al., 1999; Shrivastava, 1995b; Stead and Stead, 1995). Much of this research has been normative in focus, focusing on improving "eco-efficiency" and understanding and predicting why and how corporations "can take steps forward toward [being] environmentally more sustainable" (Starik and Marcus, 2000: 542).

Within this existing path, the research foci discussed in chapter 3 offer multiple avenues for inquiry, each building on rich literature that plots its course. On the whole, these streams apply existing theories and models as a means to understand the complex relationships between business and the natural environment. B&NE research within the domains of organizational behavior, strategy, marketing and operations will continue on paths set since the mid-1990s and before. We can also expect increased attention in both the disciplinary and topical domains on which this scholarship is built.

As noted earlier, research productivity in the disciplines of accounting, finance and information technology (IT) have been notably low. Why is this so? Are the editors of the journals in these fields uninterested in the topic? Does the empirical domain fail to provide an avenue for theoretical contributions within these disciplines? Presumably not. It is far more likely that other issues or challenges within these literatures have dominated attention as defined research precedent. However, as the salience of environmental concerns continues to grow more broadly, the world economy struggles to recover from its collapse in 2008 (Stiglitz, 2009) and information technology continues its rapid development, we expect that the accounting, finance and IT disciplines will come to address B&NE issues more fully. Emergent research on weather derivatives (Dessai and Hulme, 2004; Randalls, 2010), carbon accounting (Mackenzie, 2009), the role of full reserve banking (Røpke, 2017) and information systems innovation for environmental sustainability (Melville, 2012) indicates that this is, indeed, happening.

Beyond this disciplinary expansion, growth can also be seen in topical domains that have not generally received significant attention within the business literature, despite their environmental and economic importance. New research has begun to focus on eco-tourism (Lee and Moscardo, 2005), agriculture (Weber, Heinze and DeSoucey, 2008) and construction (Henn and Hoffman, 2013). As well, new streams of research include attention to new roles of the firm and Base of the Pyramid strategies (London and Hart, 2004; Nidumolu, Prahalad and Rangaswami, 2009), as well to new kinds of market models, such as regenerative capitalism, collaborative consumption, sharing economy, shared value, conscious capitalism and flourishing (Ehrenfeld, 2004; Fullerton, 2015; Harmari et al., 2016).

Overall, this work leaves unchallenged the underlying tensions of the market economy. It treats environmental issues as standard market or business phenomena, often representing them within the literature as a market shift. Market pressures bring sustainability to business attention through core management channels and functions including: coercive drivers – in the form of domestic and international regulations and the courts; resource drivers – from suppliers, buyers, shareholders, investors, banks and insurance companies; market drivers – from consumers, trade associations, competitors and consultants; and social drivers – from non-profit organizations, activist groups, the press, religious institutions and academia (Hoffman, 2000). Corporate responses continue to require examination in the areas of: organization and culture, framing and discourse, individual and managerial perceptions, disclosure and reporting, multi-national corporations, clean-tech and entrepreneurship, supply chain management and industrial ecology.

Research is geared towards helping companies improve competitive positioning by linking environmental and corporate strategy. This involves translating the issue into the core literatures discussed in this book, including: financial performance, competitive strategy, resource-based view, institutional theory, stakeholder theory, management and critical theory. In each case, we have established models and language that can be used to conceptualize the issue and formulate research. In this way, sustainability becomes much like any other business research issue caused by a market shift. Market expectations change and technological developments advance, leaving certain industries to adapt or face demise while others rise to fill their place in the long-accepted notion of "creative destruction" (Schumpeter, 1994). Efforts in this research direction have an important role in seeking to understand business activities as they relate to the environment in the present context. However, we must also recognize that this context is changing.

The Anthropocene as a discontinuity

There is growing concern that the dominant strands of B&NE research are ill-suited to the emergent environmental problems of the twenty-first century. Indeed, some suggest that the contemporary conceptualization of "sustainability" has been subverted by corporate interests such that it has lost its meaning and does not go far enough as presently envisaged (Sandelands and Hoffman, 2008; Welford, 1997). It has become merely a label for strategies actually driven by standard economic and institutional mechanisms (Delmas and Burbano, 2011; Jacobs, 1993). According to Gladwin (2012: 657), "The past half-century has been marked by an exponential explosion of environmental knowledge, technology, regulation, education, awareness, and organizations. But none of this has served to diminish the flow of terrifying scientific warnings about the fate of the planet." So, while the ongoing B&NE research into "greening" the market and business is a good thing, it is not enough. We are now facing a suite of environmental challenges that are unlike anything we have ever seen before. We are now living in what some scientists call the Anthropocene, a proposed, post-Holocene geologic epoch – the "age of humans" – that acknowledges people's effect on the planet (Crutzen, 2002; Crutzen and Stoermer, 2000; Zalasiewicz et al., 2010).

The Anthropocene acknowledges that humans are now a primary operating element in the Earth's ecosystems (Crutzen and Stoermer, 2000). This idea has created an intellectual furor with a flurry of debates taking place amongst different epistemic communities (Castree, 2015). This era is argued to have started around the industrial revolution of the early 1800s, and has become more acute since the post–World War II "Great Acceleration" of resources use and pollution from around 1950 onwards (Steffen et al., 2015; Steffen, Crutzen and McNeil, 2007). It is marked by the reality that:

> Human activity has transformed between a third and a half of the land surface of the planet; Many of the world's major rivers have been dammed or diverted; Fertilizer plants produce more nitrogen than is fixed naturally by all terrestrial ecosystems; Humans use more than half of the world's readily accessible freshwater runoff.
>
> (Crutzen, 2002: 23)

Although there is some disagreement amongst Earth Scientists as to whether the Anthropocene has the mark of an epoch or a geological age (Gibbard and Walker, 2014), it is said to represent "a new phase in the history of both humankind and of the Earth, when natural forces and human forces became intertwined, so that the fate of one determines the fate of the other. Geologically, this is a remarkable episode in the history of this planet" (Zalasiewicz et al., 2010).

Whilst much work is being done within the Anthropocene Working Group in ratifying the Anthropocene as a unit in the official geological time scale, another group of environmental scientists have sought to create more clarity on the concept by identifying key biotic and geochemical markers or "planetary boundaries" (Rockström et al., 2009; Steffen et al., 2015) that represent "thresholds below which humanity can safely operate and beyond which the stability of planetary-scale systems cannot be relied upon" (Gillings and Hagan-Lawson, 2014: 2) (see figure 4.1). Nine have been isolated: climate change, ocean acidification, ozone depletion, atmospheric aerosol loading, phosphorous and nitrogen cycles, global freshwater use, land system change, loss of biodiversity and chemical pollution (Rockström et al., 2009). "Unless there is a global catastrophe such as a meteorite impact, world war or pandemic," these planetary boundaries will continue to be approached as "mankind will remain a major environmental force for many millennia" (Crutzen, 2002: 23). Indeed, scientists believe that three have now been crossed as a result of human activity: Biosphere integrity and biogeochemical flows (nitrogen and phosphorous), climate change and species extinction (Stockholm Resilience Center, 2016).

A group of scientists, using a biotic perspective, emphasize the importance of acknowledging global "tipping points" or global scale state shifts associated with "human population growth and attendant resource consumption, habitat transformation and fragmentation, energy production and consumption, and climate change. All of these far exceed, in both rate and

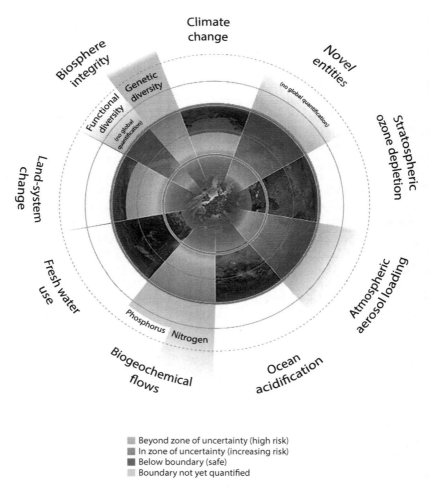

Figure 4.1 The planetary boundaries of the Anthropocene

magnitude, the forcings evident at the most recent global-scale state shift, the last glacial-interglacial transition" (Barnosky et al., 2012: 53). This will result in changes in the world's biological resources as we know them. In order to reduce the detrimental effects of rapid and unpredictable biological transformations, several systems-level shifts will be necessary: population growth and resource-use per capita must be reduced, fossil fuels must be abandoned for renewable energy sources, energy efficiency must be improved in those domains where it is not possible to phase out fossil fuels, food production must become more efficient and divergent, and biodiversity must be protected. All of these are formidable tasks.

For B&NE researchers, this acknowledgment will have profound implications for the foci and direction of our research. Most importantly, the Anthropocene Era requires us to re-order our conceptualizations of the deep entanglement of the natural and social systems, one which subverts most prior frameworks and presuppositions. Rather than fitting environmental considerations into social and economic systems, the Athropocene forces a re-ordering of B&NE frameworks. It is a statement that social systems are intruding upon natural systems to the point that natural planetary systems are now nested within social systems (Hoffman and Jennings, 2015).

This re-ordering challenges institutionalized concepts, theories and methods of B&NE research that lie within the era of environmental management. The goal of sustainable development as stated in the Rio Accord (World Commission on Environment and Development, 1987) and UN Sustainable Development Goals (2017), while laudable, becomes the wrong goal if primarily addressed within the confines of "business as usual," the efficiency gamut. Given the epochal nature of the Anthropocene and the degree and type of change it represents, this calls for more radical transformations than those provided through efficiency gains (Ehrenfeld and Hoffman, 2013). Recognition of the Anthropocene signals an urgency and complexity that much of the debate on sustainable development lacks, compelling change deep within the structures of our collective understanding of the social and natural world around us (Nyberg and Wright, 2016).

> The Anthropocene is not a problem for which there can be a solution. Rather, it names an emergent set of geo-social conditions that already fundamentally structure the horizon of human existence. It is thus not a new factor that can be accommodated within existing conceptual frameworks, including those within which policy is developed, but signals a profound shift in the human relation to the planet that questions the very foundations of these frameworks themselves.
>
> (Rowan, 2014: 9)

Some even go so far as to argue that capitalism itself is sowing the seeds of our own destruction (Wright and Nyberg, 2015; 2016).

B&NE research in the era of the Anthropocene

Recognition of the Anthropocene has broad implications for how we think about business sustainability, and whether this, indeed, can be considered in isolation. Rather than fitting sustainability into the existing models of the market, B&NE research must recognize that the ways in which existing markets have been designed have led to an appropriation of natural systems with potentially catastrophic consequences (Hoffman and Jennings, 2015; MacKenzie, 2009). Where the past incarnation of B&NE research incorporated the issue within existing business logics and models, the next iteration focuses on changes within those logics and models themselves, focusing on systemic changes in market architectures (Fligstein, 2001) and prompting a re-examination of the role of the corporation in society (Hoffman, 2017). The dramatic and uncertain futures associated with the Anthropocene – with the reaching of various planetary boundaries – represent a critique of the existing policies and ways of doing business. The B&NE field needs to shift from research focused on reducing unsustainability to that of focusing on creating sustainability (Ehrenfeld, 2008).

This shift represents a profoundly provocative turn. The accompanying tensions that it will create can be vividly observed in the currently polarized debate over climate change in the United States, one of the planetary boundaries of the Anthropocene (Hoffman, 2015, 2011b; Lefsrud and Meyer, 2012; Hulme, 2009). But, it is the issue of climate change, more than any other, that has triggered the shift to the fourth wave of B&NE research shown in figure 2.2. Where the models of prior waves do not challenge the underlying models of B&NE research, the fourth wave forces such an examination. No longer can we treat the environment as a limitless source of materials and a limitless sink for waste (Daly, 1991; 1993) or leave unquestioned the notion that perpetual economic growth based on continued consumption is desirable or even possible. B&NE research in the Anthropocene calls for new models that supplant these old ways of thinking and new metrics to act as guideposts for successful outcomes (Hoffman and Ehrenfeld, 2015). The fourth wave is a departure from the dominant models of economics and management science, recognizing that we are dealing with an impact on the environment that goes far beyond our standard notions of environmental issues as externalities or occasional instances of market failure (Callon, 1998). This departure may yield new forms of research in several domains. Below, we will offer eight domains for further research, but the notion of the Anthropocene is so disruptive as to yield opportunities for many more.

Challenge foundational models of the market economy

Some prior B&NE research has tended to reproduce specific understandings of what are desirable activities and responses to societies' environmental issues by abstracting or disentangling the environmentally damaging activities from the everyday practices in which they are embedded. In this way, they (inadvertently) overlook what may keep these activities in place. Taken together, these features could provide a possible explanation for why, despite increased knowledge about what needs to be done and how changes can be brought about, many environmental problems continue not only to persist, but to grow.

But, B&NE research within the Anthropocene challenges prior research models that rest on eco-modernistic assumptions (Hajer, 1996). This creates an opportunity to ask deeper questions about some underlying assumptions of the capitalist model, one in which efficiency improvements are generally considered a good thing. In prior B&NE research, there has been little consideration or questioning of whether existing business activities are, indeed, sustainable in the long run. For example, there is a growing need for research that challenges the underlying economic premise of individualism (particularly with regard to consumerism), the purpose of the firm being to make money for shareholders (Stoudt, 2012), and the existence of externalities as a pervasive rather than occasional form of market failure (Callon, 1998; Ehrenfeld, 2008).

Questioning standard models and metrics

As part of this critique of traditional market systems, B&NE research in the era of the Anthropocene prompts a re-examination of the models used to understand and explain the market, particularly neo-classical economics (Beinhocker and Hanauer, 2014) and principal-agent theory (Stoudt, 2012), both of which are built on rather dismal simplifications of human beings as largely untrustworthy and driven by avarice, greed and selfishness. There is an acute need to move beyond text-book economics and finance, and explore the limitations of sacrosanct metrics, such as discount rates (Stern, 2009) and Gross Domestic Product (Stiglitz, Sen and Fitoussi, 2015; Kubiszewski et al, 2013), by considering the ways in which these metrics limit efforts at addressing social and environmental sustainability.

Expand existing management theories and literatures

Beyond a critique of neo-classical economics and agency theory, the Anthropocene creates opportunities to expand existing management disciplines by bringing them more in line with bio-physical realities. For example, most research disproportionately directs attention to those with "voice" in deciding what business can and should do. For example, institutional theory and its depictions of the field tend to bias towards formal structures of power. In other words, it focuses on the elites of society that have the power to project and protect their interests within field level debates. These elites define the issues and develop the solutions. But the impacts of contemporary environmental problems (like climate change) will be felt across the social spectrum, with differential impacts on the poor, disenfranchised and disconnected. Elites of rich countries, for example, will be far more able to adapt to the impacts of climate change than those in the low-lying areas of developing countries (i.e. Bangladesh) or poorer cities (i.e. New Orleans). But a bias towards developed country elites creates a blind spot to considering issues of equity, fairness and environmental justice in institutional outcomes (Bullard, 2005; Taylor, 2000), one that is compounded with its inability to recognize the interests of future generations (Lovbrand et al., 2015). Management theory will only take notice of such groups when they are sufficiently aggrieved and able to amass the requisite power to voice their concerns. But certainly, foresight of such environmentally induced aggrievements is important for understanding the emergence of social instability, social movement mobilization and institutional action.

Additionally, B&NE research ignores the "interests" of a non-social actor – the natural environment – within what are inherently social models. Instead, particularly within the stakeholder and social movement literatures, social actors interpret, assess and represent the interests of the natural environment. In the present context, scientists and environmental NGOs are playing a role in articulating the concerns over climate change and other natural environment problems (Lefsrud and Meyer, 2012; Hoffman, 2015). The contested nature of these debates and the willingness of some to discount or outright reject the results of scientific analyses that contradict their worldview leaves the B&NE field woefully under-theorized by excluding the presence of the natural environment which can destabilize economic systems through systems collapses related to storms, sea-level rise, species extinction and other means.

Foster greater links between natural and business systems

One answer to this tension is to foster more research that links social and environmental systems. While most theories and models of organizational action offer only loose connections between these realms (Gladwin, Kennelly and Krause, 1995), there are examples of B&NE research that has sought to correct this deficiency by depicting the biosphere (including the sinks, sources and drivers of ecosystems health) as the domain that encompasses economic, organizational and social activity (Hawken, 1993; Jennings and Zandbergen, 1995; Latour, 2004; Lovelock, 2000). There are others calling for moves to integrate environmental considerations into human systems in order to avoid the anthropogenic calamities of continued economic growth (Daly, 1977; 1991; 1996; Urhammer and Røpke, 2013).

Whiteman et al. (forthcoming) suggest that we reframe the planetary boundaries from the physical sciences into Key Performance Indicators (KPIs) of the planet within the management sciences.

Expanded opportunities in critical theory

The Anthropocene creates an opening for more challenges from critical management and actor network theory approaches, conducting research that is based on the premise that the natural and social systems are constitutively entangled and that ignoring these entanglements would be willful negligence (Latour, 2013). The Anthropocene brings considerations for "sustainability" into a new orientation, one that requires adjustments of socio-economic systems to the limits set by the biosphere in recognition of the planetary boundaries beyond which social systems should not go, but already have (see figure 4.1). Climate change, droughts, wildfires, food insecurity, water scarcity and the social unrest that results: these are all emergent markers of the Anthropocene that point to a fundamental system failure created by our social and economic structures.

Policy development

The complexities of the Earth System's processes and feedbacks are what underpin the planet's resilience and at the same time makes it vulnerable to small change "tipping" developments (Barnosky et al., 2012; Rockström et al., 2009), which can transform the very conditions for life as we know it. The potency and uncertainty of these developments call for policies that are far more ecologically attuned than existing environmental and economic policies. For instance, to fully address the global issue of climate change, society and the markets must be designed to go carbon neutral – and then carbon negative. This cannot be done by employing business models that are built upon the single company focus of prior research streams or within the existing market structures. Although some argue that carbon markets are inherently flawed (Lohmann, 2005), it is unlikely that the "market system" will be eliminated in the future. It is, therefore, necessary to address how carbon and other markets can be re-designed with the aim of de-carbonizing the economy, protecting biodiversity, ensuring freshwater provisioning and otherwise stay within the planetary boundaries defined by scientists. The implications of this kind of policy regime for international, national and local governance are far from clear, and implementing these policies is by no means a straightforward endeavor. Future environmental policy must do more than regulate the existing, it must also facilitate transitions to sustainable futures.

Systems framing

Sustainability is a property of the system as a whole; not of just one firm. The notion of an energy company installing a windfarm and calling itself sustainable makes no empirical sense (Ehrenfeld and Hoffman, 2013). A more sustainable energy system incorporates the whole grid, encompassing generation, transmission, distribution, use and mobility. Although there is a substantial body of energy system research documenting that it is technically possible to achieve the necessary low-carbon energy system transformation (European Commission, 2011; Pregger et al., 2013), the organizational and institutional challenges that this kind of systems thinking introduces and the implications it has for policy and business is markedly less researched. Systemic transformations are contentious processes; research needs to document and explain these developments.

One could contend that research on greening of the supply chain seeks to broaden B&NE research on the impact and action of each firm to include its network connections to other organizations, notably suppliers, buyers, customers, regulators, banks and others. Much of this research focuses primarily on optimizing material flows and supply chain logistics, without substantial changes in overall system purposes and foundations. While there is growing research interest in full supply chain accounting involving the use of life-cycle analysis (Zamagni et al., 2012), industrial ecology (Ayres and Ayres, 2002) and circular economy (Bocken, de Pauw, Bakker and van der Grinten, 2016), new research into the models that underlie both production and consumption systems is needed. Without a reduction in consumption and a re-examination of both needs and wants, a human population that is expected to grow from 7.5 billion today to 10 billion by 2050 cannot stay within planetary boundaries.

Expanding the systems approach, B&NE research in the era of the Anthropocene requires a breakdown or even elimination of the dichotomy between humans and nature with consideration for its scientific, social, economic and ethical dimensions (Oldfield et al., 2014). To this end, some behavioral social scientists have worked on specific boundaries of the Anthropocene, others have attempted to link across them, conceptually and empirically, to social systems. Whiteman et al. (2013) reviewed some of these efforts and offered a Planetary Boundaries framework for mapping the nine planetary boundaries. While this framework is important for analyzing the consequences of corporate behavior more work is necessary to link the Planetary Boundaries framework to the market behavior of firms to consider what and how they produce in relation to these boundaries. Such systems modeling will, by nature, have to consider ecological limits in the context of tipping points and regenerative capacity (Baue and McElroy, 2013; Krabbe et al., 2015).

New organizational structures and forms of governance

As corporate activity expands into new domains, with linkages to complex systems of actors through broader networks and supply chains, new forms of organization also emerge. Already, data show that the vertically integrated, shareholder-owned corporation is in rapid decline as a corporate model, with half as many public corporations in 2012 as there were in 1997 as they are superseded by alternative forms of organizing (Davis, 2013). Though not new, other forms, such as Cooperatives, or Employee-Owned Companies are part of a movement that consider more than the shareholder in defining the actions of a corporation (Davis, 2013). Similarly, hybrid organizations are emerging at the intervening space between the for-profit and non-profit sectors and strive to merge the institutional logics of each domain (Battilana and Dorado, 2010). Alternatively described as Fourth Sector, Blended Value, For-Benefit, Values-Driven, Mission-Driven, or B-Corporations (Boyd et al., 2009), hybrid organizations present a bridge between two ends of a dichotomy previously seen as incommensurable; economic profit and social and environmental mission (Hoffman and Haigh, 2011).

This work includes attention to new forms of NGO-business partnerships (Kong et al., 2002), public-private partnerships for the environment (Koppenjan and Enserink, 2009) and local-global associations of heterogeneous actors (Georg and Irwin, 2002). The underlying ambition of much of this work is to examine how new development paths are being created (Karnøe and Garud, 2012). This includes new forms of governance that can enable a move to a low-carbon society (Kolk and Pinske, 2004; Levy and Kolk, 2002), what some authors have dubbed sustainable transition management (Kemp, Schot and Hoogma, 1998; Shove and Walker, 2010; Smith, Stirling and Berkhout, 2005).

And finally, emergent areas of B&NE research include work in positive organizational studies (POS) and positive psychology (Dutton and Glynn, 2008). Both domains are grounded in the core concept of flourishing. Where sustainability holds "the possibility that human and other life will flourish on the planet forever" (Ehrenfeld, 2008: 6), POS holds for the possibility of "conditions that foster flourishing at the individual, work group, and organizational levels" (Dutton and Glynn, 2008). The linkage between social and natural flourishing is clear and the research paths it opens up are many and varied in realizing the fullest human potential (Hoffman and Haigh, 2011).

The fluid future of B&NE research

In sum, these are just eight broad streams in which B&NE research can explore sustainable business in the era of the Anthropocene. As standard business models are questioned, new ones can emerge as possible augmentation or replacement. We are in a period of "revolutionary science" (Kuhn, 1970) where the old models and theories used to explain the connection between business and natural systems are no longer complete. New models, such as regenerative capitalism (Fullerton, 2015), the collaborative economy (Owyang, Tran and Silva, 2013), conflict-free sourcing (Young, 2015) and the sharing economy (Hamari, Sjöklint and Ukkonen, 2016) are emerging as contenders for the next period of "normal science." The role of B&NE research in this period of flux is to help speed the process of paradigmatic change by conducting research that enlightens our way forward.

5 Conclusion

B&NE research has established more than a 20-year foundation of scholarly output, with trajectories showing an upward trend until the late 2000s (see figure 2.1) followed by a plateau (see figures 2.4–2.6). As we look to the future, we can expect continued work within both the mainstream literature and the specialty journals, and on both existing research streams as well as new and contradictory streams. This duality of being both on the "inside" and on the "outside" is critical to the growth and vitality of the field. It represents a healthy tension of focusing on environmental issues within the existing models, theories and paradigms of "normal science" (Kuhn, 1970) to contribute to the field while also stepping outside the domains of existing theory to fully capture the magnitude and scope of the problem we face by pushing "the literature to ask the 'big' questions and push beyond the existing paradigm" (Hoffman and Bansal, 2012: 21) that are built on a model of "revolutionary" science (Kuhn, 1970).

Certainly there is a need for both. The first helps to bring existing theories into more close alignment with biophysical reality and seeks to mitigate the impact we are having on the environment. It also helps scholars to succeed and, in turn, become themselves "sustainable" (and maintain legitimacy within the academy through publication, promotion and tenure) by building upon the models and theories of the academic craft with rigorous analysis. The second recognizes that, despite the growing research on environmental issues, the environment continues to worsen with growing concerns for climate change, water depletion, species extinction, habitat destruction and a recognition of the Anthropocene. The complexity, uncertainty and ambiguity of which justifies a more pronounced engagement of B&NE research. This focus will re-energize and re-radicalize the field (Gladwin, 2012; Starik and Kanashiro, 2013), returning to the more critical tone of B&NE research from 20 years ago, when scholars of environmental issues resided outside of mainstream scholarship and practice by criticizing and challenging the underlying institutions of the field. Rather than merely fitting B&NE research within existing management theories and models, this new work will explore the ways in which the fundamental systems of thinking and beliefs must adapt to the present-day reality of the Anthropocene.

The goal for forward-looking B&NE scholars is to do both and in so doing, advance management theory and address the implications of the shift to the Anthropocene. As a result, B&NE research holds a special vantage point from which to examine those theories for possible alteration and adjustment in the face of an anomaly that highlights the extent to which these existing theories are no longer adequate. And in this way, B&NE research holds a critical key for invigorating and revitalizing the broader field of management research of which it is a part.

References

Aguilera, R., Rupp, D., Williams, C. and Ganapathi, J. (2007). "Putting the S back in corporate social responsibility: A multi-level theory of social change in organizations," *Academy of Management Review*, 32(3): 836–863.

Ahi, P. and Searcy, C. (2013). "A comparative literature analysis of definitions for green and sustainable supply chain management," *Journal of Cleaner Production*, 52: 329–341.

Andersson, L. and Bateman, T. (2000). "Individual environmental initiative: Championing natural environmental issues in US business organizations," *Academy of Management Journal*, 43(4): 548–570.

Ángel del Brio, J. and Junquera, B. (2003). "A review of the literature on environmental innovation management in SMEs: Implications for public policies," *Technovation*, 23(12): 939–948.

Ansell, C. and Vogel, D. (2006). *What's the Beef: The Contested Governance of European Food Safety* (Cambridge, MA: MIT Press).

Aragón-Correa, J. (1998). "Strategic proactivity and firm approach to the natural environment," *Academy of Management Journal*, 41(5): 556–567.

Aragón-Correa, J. and Sharma, S. (2003). "A contingent resource-based view of proactive corporate environmental strategy," *Academy of Management Review*, 28(1):71–88.

Arts, B. (2002). "Green alliances of business and NGOs. New styles of self-regulation or dead-end roads?" *Corporate Social Responsibility and Environmental Management*, 9(1): 26–36.

Ashford, N. (1993). "Understanding technological responses of industrial firms to environmental problems: Implications for government policy," in K. Fischer and J. Schot (eds.), *Environmental Strategies for Industry: International Perspectives on Research Needs and Policy Implications* (Washington, DC: Island Press): 277–307.

Ashford, N., Ayres, C. and Stone, R. F. (1985). "Using regulation to change the market for innovation," *Harvard Environmental Law Review*, 9(2):419–466.

Ayres, R. (1997). "The life-cycle of chlorine, part I: Chlorine production and the chlorine-mercury connection," *Journal of Industrial Ecology*, 1(1): 81–94.

Ayres, R. and Ayres, L. (eds.). (2002). *Handbook of Industrial Ecology* (Northampton, MA: Edward Elgar Publishing, Inc.).

Baas, L. and Boon, F. (2007). "The introduction and dissemination of industrial symbiosis projects in the Rotterdam Harbour and Industrial Complex," *International Journal of Environmental Technology and Management*, 7(5–6): 551–577.

Banerjee, S. B. (2001). "Managerial perceptions of corporate environmentalism: Interpretations from industry and strategic implications for organizations," *Journal of Management Studies*, 38(4): 489–513.

Banerjee, S. B. (2003). "Who sustains whose development? Sustainable development and the reinvention of nature," *Organization Studies*, 24(1): 143–180.

Banerjee, S. B. (2008). "Corporate social responsibility: The good, the bad and the ugly," *Critical Sociology*, 34(1): 51–79.

Banerjee, S. B. (2012). "Critical perspectives on business and the natural environment," in P. Bansal and A. Hoffman (eds.), *The Oxford Handbook on Business and the Natural Environment* (Oxford, UK: Oxford University Press): 572–590.

Bansal, P. (2003) "From issues to actions: The importance of individual concerns and organizational values in responding to natural environmental issues," *Organization Science*, 14(5): 510–527.

Bansal, P. and Clelland, I. (2004). "Talking trash: Legitimacy, impression management, and unsystematic risk in the context of the natural environment," *Academy of Management Journal*, 47(1): 197–218.

Bansal, P. and Gao, J. (2006). "Building the future by looking to the past: Examining research published on organizations and the environment," *Organization & Environment*, 19(4): 458–478.

Bansal, P. and Hoffman, A. (eds.). (2012). *The Oxford Handbook on Business and the Natural Environment* (Oxford, UK: Oxford University Press).

Bansal, P. and Roth, K. (2000). "Why companies go green: A model of ecological responsiveness," *Academy of Management Journal*, 43: 717–736.

Barnett, M., Darnall, N. and Husted, B. (2015). "Sustainability strategy in constrained economic times," *Long Range Planning*, 48(2): 63–68.

Barnett, M. and King, A. (2008). "Good fences make good neighbors: A longitudinal analysis of an industry self-regulatory institution," *Academy of Management Journal*, 51(6): 1150–1170.

Barnett, M. and Salomon, R. (2006). "Beyond dichotomy: The curvilinear relationship between social responsibility and financial performance," *Strategic Management Journal*, 27(11): 1101–1122.

Barnosky A. et al. (2012). "Approaching a state shift in Earth's biosphere." *Nature*, 486: 52–58.

Battilana, J. and Dorado, S. (2010). "Building sustainable hybrid organizations: The case of commercial microfinance organizations." *Academy of Management Journal*, 53(6): 1419–1440.

Baue, B. and McElroy, M. (2013). "Research needs and opportunities in context-based sustainability." *Financial Reporting*, 2, 47–70.

Bazerman, M. and Hoffman, A. (1999). "Sources of environmentally destructive behavior: Individual, organizational and institutional perspectives," *Research in Organizational Behavior*, 21: 39–79.

Beamon, B. (1999). "Measuring supply chain performance," *International Journal of Operations & Production Management*, 19(3): 275–292.

Beinhocker, E. and Hanauer, N. (2014). "Redefining capitalism," *McKinsey Quarterly*, 3(3): 160–169.

Beinhocker, E. and Hanauer, N. (2014). "Redefining capitalism," *McKinsey Quarterly*, September.

Bennett, M. and James, P. (eds.) (1998). *The Green Bottom Line: Environmental Accounting for Management* (Sheffield: Greenleaf Publishing).

Bergström, O. and Diedrich, A. (2011). "Exercising social responsibility in downsizing: Enrolling and mobilizing actors at a Swedish high-tech company," *Organization Studies*, 32(7): 897–919.

Bergström, O. and Dobers, P. (2000). "Organizing sustainable development: From diffusion to translation," *Sustainable Development*, 8: 167–179.

Berman, S., Wicks, A., Kotha, S. and Jones, T. (1999). "Does stakeholder orientation matter? The relationship between stakeholder management models and firm financial performance," *Academy of Management Journal*, 42(5):488–506.

Bertels, S., Hoffman, A. and DeJordy, R. (2014) "The varied work of challenger movements: Identifying challenger roles in the U.S. environmental movement," *Organization Studies*, 35(8): 1171–1210.

Bhattacharya, C. B. and Sen, S. (2003). "Consumer-company identification: A framework for understanding consumers' relationships with companies," *Journal of Marketing*, 67(4): 76–88.

Bjørn, A., Bey, N., Georg, S., Røpke, I. and Hauschild, M. Z. (2017). "Is Earth recognized as a finite system in corporate responsibility reporting?" *Journal of Cleaner Production*, 163: 106–117.

Bjørner, T., Hansen, L. and Russell, C. (2004). "Environmental labeling and consumers' choice: An empirical analysis of the effect of the Nordic Swan," *Journal of Environmental Economics and Management*, 47(3): 411–434.

Bocken, N. M., de Pauw, I., Bakker, C., & van der Grinten, B. (2016). "Product design and business model strategies for a circular economy," *Journal of Industrial and Production Engineering*, 33(5): 308–320.

Bocken, N. M., Olivetti, E. A., Cullen, J. M., Potting, J. and Lifset, R. (2017). "Taking circularity to the next level," *Journal of Industrial Ecology*, 21(3): 476–482.

Boons, F. and Baas, L. (1997). "Types of industrial ecology: The problem of coordination," *Journal of Cleaner Production*, 5(1–2):79–86.

Boons, F. and Strannegård, L. (2000). "Organizations coping with their natural environment: A laboratory for institutionalization," *International Studies of Management & Organization*, 30(3): 7–17.

Boons, F. and Wagner, M. (2009). "Assessing the relationship between economic and ecological performance: Distinguishing system levels and the role of innovation," *Ecological Economics*, 68: 1908–1914.

Bowen, F., Cousins, P. D., Lamming, R. C. and Faruk, A. C. (2001). "The role of supply management capabilities in green supply," *Production and Operations Management*, 10(2): 174–189.

Boyd, B., Henning, N., Reyna, E., Wang, D. and Welch, M. (2009). *Hybrid Organizations: New Business Models for Environmental Leadership* (Sheffield: Greenleaf Publishing).

Bullard, R. (2005). *Quest for Environmental Justice* (San Francisco, CA: Sierra Club Books).

Buysse, K. and Verbeke, A. (2003). "Proactive environmental strategies: A stake-holder management perspective," *Strategic Management Journal*, 24: 453–470.

Callon, M. (1986). "Some elements of a sociology of translation: Domestication of the scallops and the fishermen of St Brieuc Bay," in J. Law (eds.), *Power, Action and Belief: A New Sociology of Knowledge* (London: Routledge and Kegan Paul): 196–233.

Callon, M. (1998). "An essay on framing and overflowing: Economic externalities revisied by Sociology," in M. Callon (ed.), *The Laws of the Market* (London: Blackwell Publishers/The Sociological Review): 244–269.

Callon, M. (2009). "Civilizing markets: Carbon trading between in vitro and in vivo experiments," *Accounting, Organizations and Society*, 34(3–4): 535–548.

Carroll, A. (1979). "A three-dimensional conceptual model of corporate performance," *Academy of Management Review*, 4:497–505.

Carter, C., Clegg, S. and Wåhlin, N. (2011). "When science meets strategic realpolitik: The case of the Copenhagen UN climate change summit," *Critical Perspectives on Accounting*, 22(7): 682–697.

Castleman, B. (1987). "International mobility of hazardous products, industries and wastes," *International Journal of Health Services*, 17(4): 617–633.

Castree, N. (2015). "Changing the Antropo(s)cene: Geographers, global environmental change and the politics of knowledge," *Dialogues in Human Geography*, 5(3): 301–316.

Catton, W. and Dunlap, R. (1980). "A new ecological paradigm for post-exuberant society," *American Behavioral Scientist*, 24(1): 15–47.

Chertow, M. (2007). "Uncovering industrial symbiosis," *Journal of Industrial Ecology*, 11(1): 11–30.

Cho, C., Roberts, R. and Patten, D. (2010). "The language of U.S. corporate environmental disclosure," *Accounting, Organizations and Society*, 35(4): 431–443.

Christmann, P. (2000). "Effects of 'best practices' on environmental management on cost advantage: The role of complementary assets," *Academy of Management Journal*, 43(4): 663–680.

Christmann, P., and Taylor, G. (2001). "Globalization and the environment: Determinants of firm self-regulation in China," *Journal of International Business Studies*, 32(3): 439–458.

Clapp, J. (2002). "What the pollution haven debate overlooks," *Global Environmental Policy*, 2(2): 11–19.

Clarke, B. (2017). "Rethinking Gaia: Stengers, Latour, Margulis," *Theory, Culture & Society*, 34(4): 3–26.

Clarkson, M. (1995). "A stakeholder framework for analyzing and evaluating corporate social performance," *Academy of Management Review*, 20: 92–117.

Coglianese, C. (2001). "Social movements, law, and society: The institutionalization of the environmental movement," *University of Pennsylvania Law Review*, 150: 85–118.

Corbett, C. and DeCroix, G. (2001). "Shared-savings contracts for indirect materials in supply chains: Channel profits and environmental impacts," *Management Science*, 47(7): 881–893.

Corbett, C. and Kirsch, D. (2001). "International diffusion of ISO 14000 certification," *Production and Operations Management*, 10(3): 327–342.

Costanza, R., d'Arge, R., de Groot, R., Farber, S., Grasso, M., Hannon, B., Naeem, S., Limburg, K., Paruelo, J., O'Neill, R., Raskin, R., Sutton, P. and van den Belt, M. (1997). "The value of the world's ecosystem services and natural capital," *Nature*, 387: 253–260.

Crane, A., Matten, D. and Moon, J. (2008). "Ecological citizenship and the corporation: Politicizing the new corporate environmentalism," *Organization & Environment*, 21(4): 371–389.

Crutzen, P. (2002). "Geology of mankind," *Nature*, 415: 23.

Crutzen, P. and Stoermer, E. (2000). "The 'Anthropocene,'" *Global Change Newsletter*, 41: 17–18.

Cyert, R. and March, J. (1992). *A Behavioral Theory of the Firm* (Cambridge, MA: Wiley-Blackwell).

Czarniawska, B. (2009). "Commentary: STS Meets MOS," *Organization*, 16(1), 155–160.

Czarniawska, B. and Sevón, G. (eds.). (1996). *Translating Organizational Change* (Berlin: Walter de Gruyter).

Dahlmann, F. and Brammer, S. (2011). "Exploring and explaining patterns of adoption and selection in corporate environmental strategies in the USA," *Organization Studies*, 32(4): 527–553.

Daly, H. (1991) [1977]. *Steady-State Economics* (2nd ed.). (Washington, DC: Island Press).

Daly, H. (1993). "The perils of free trade," *Scientific American*, November: 50–57.

Daly, H. (1996). *Beyond Growth: The Economics of Sustainable Development* (Boston: Beacon Press).

Darnall, N. and Sides, S. (2008). "Assessing the performance of voluntary environmental programs: Does certification matter?" *Policy Studies Journal*, 36(1): 95–117.

Davis, G. (2013). "After the corporation," *Politics & Society*, 41(2): 283–308.

Dean, T. and McMullen, J. (2007). "Toward a theory of sustainable entrepreneurship: Reducing environmental degradation through entrepreneurial action," *Journal of Business Venturing*, 22(1): 50–76.

Deegan, C. (2002). "The legitimising effect of social and environmental disclosures: A theoretical foundation," *Accounting, Auditing and Accountability Journal*, 15(2): 282–311.

Delmas, M. (2001). "Stakeholders and competitive advantage: The case of ISO 14001," *Production and Operations Management*, 10(3): 343–358.

Delmas, M. (2002). "The diffusion of environmental management standards in Europe and in the United States: An institutional perspective," *Policy Sciences*, 35(1): 91–119.

Delmas, M. and Burbano, V. (2011). "The drivers of greenwashing," *California Management Review*, 54(1): 64–87.

Delmas, M., Hoffmann, V. and Kuss, M. (2011). "Under the tip of the iceberg: Absoptive capacity, environmental strategy, and competitive advantage," *Business & Society*, 50(1): 116–154.

Delmas, M. and Montes-Sancho, M. J. (2010). "Voluntary agreements to improve environmental quality: symbolic and substantive cooperation," *Strategic Management Journal*, 31: 575–560.

Delmas, M. and Toffel, M. (2004). "Stakeholders and environmental management practices: An institutional framework," *Business Strategy & the Environment*, 13(4): 209–222.

Delmas, M. and Toffel, M. (2008). "Organizational responses to environmental demands: Opening the black box," *Strategic Management Journal*, 29(10): 1027–1055.

Dessai, S. and Hulme, M. (2004). "Does climate adaption policy need probabilities?" *Climate Policy*, 4(2): 107–128.

DiMaggio, P. (1988). "Interest and agency in institutional theory," in L. Zucker (ed.), *Institutional Patterns and Organizations* (Cambridge, MA: Ballinger): 3–21.

Ditz, D., Ranganathan, J. and Banks, R. (1995). *Green Ledgers: Case Studies in Corporate Environmental Accounting* (Baltimore, MD: World Resources Institute).

Dixon, S. and Clifford, A. (2007). "Ecopreneurship: A new approach to managing the triple bottom line," *Journal of Organizational Change Management*, 20(3): 326–345.

Doganova, L. and Karnøe, P. (January 2015). "Building markets for clean technologies: Controversies, environmental concerns and economic worth," *Industrial Marketing Management*, 44: 22–31.

Doh, J. and Guay, T. (2006). "Corporate social responsibility, public policy, and NGO activism in Europe and the United States: An institutional-stakeholder perspective," *Journal of Management Studies*, 43(1): 47–73.

Douglas, T. (2007). "Reporting on the triple bottom line at Cascade Engineering," *Global Business & Organizational Excellence*, 26(3): 35–43.

Dowell, G., Hart, S. and Yeung, B. (2000) "Do corporate global environmental standards create or destroy market value?" *Management Science*, 46(8): 1059–1076.

Downs, A. (1972) "Up and down with ecology: The issue-attention cycle," *Public Interest*, 28: 38–50.

Drysek, J. (1997). *The Politics of the Earth: Environmental Discourses* (New York: Oxford University Press).

Dutton, J. and Glynn, M. (2008). "Positive organizational scholarship," in J. Barling and C. Cooper (eds.), *The SAGE Handbook of Organizational Behavior* (Los Angeles: Sage): 693–712.

Eccles, R. and Saltzman, D. (2011). "Achieving sustainability through integrated reporting," *Stanford Social Innovation Review*, Summer: 56–61.

Egri, C. and Herman, S. (2000). "Leadership in the North American environmental sector: Values, leadership styles, and contexts of environmental leaders and their organizations," *Academy of Management Journal*, 43(4): 571–604.

Egri, C. and Pinfield, L. (1996). "Organizations and the biosphere: Ecologies and environments," In S. Clegg, C. Hardy. and W. Nord (eds.), *Handbook of Organization Studies* (London: Sage Publications): 459–483.

Ehrenfeld, J. (1997) "Industrial ecology: A new framework for product and process design," *Journal of Cleaner Production*, 5(1–2): 87–95.

Ehrenfeld, J. (2004). "Searching for sustainability: No quick fix," *Reflections*, 5(8): 1–13.

Ehrenfeld, J. (2008). *Sustainability by Design: A Subversive Strategy for Transforming Our Consumer Culture* (New Haven, CT: Yale University Press).

Ehrenfeld, J. and Gertler, N. (1997). "Industrial ecology in practice: The evolution of interdependence at Kalundborg," *Journal of Industrial Ecology*, 1(1): 67–79.

Ehrenfeld, J. and Hoffman, A. (2013). *Flourishing: A Frank Conversation on Sustainability* (Palo Alto, CA: Stanford University Press).

Ehrlich, P. and Ehrlich, A. (1991). *The Population Explosion* (New York: Simon & Schuster).

Elkington, J. (1999) *Cannibals with Forks: The Triple Bottom Line of 21st Century Business* (North Mankato, MN: Capstone Publishing Ltd).

Endrikat, J., Guenther, E. and Hoppe, H. (2014). "Making sense of conflicting empirical findings: A meta-analytic review of the relationship between corporate environmental and financial performance," *European Management Journal*, 32(5): 735–751.

Epstein, M. J., Buhovac, A. R. and Yuthas, K. (2015). "Managing social, environmental and financial performance simultaneously," *Long Range Planning*, 48(1): 35–45.

Eriksson, C. (2004). "Can green consumerism replace environmental regulation: A differentiated products example," *Resource and Energy Economics*, 26(3): 281–293.

Erkman, S. (1997). "Industrial ecology: An historical view," *Journal of Cleaner Production*, 5(1–2): 1–10.

Eskeland, G. and Harrison, A. (2003). "Moving to greener pastures? Multinationals and the pollution haven hypothesis," *Journal of Development Economics*, 70: 1–23.

Esty, D. and Porter, M. (1998). "Industrial ecology and competitiveness: Strategic implications for the firm," *Journal of Industrial Ecology*, 2(1): 35–43.

European Commission. (2011). *Energy Roadmap 2050*. Brussels. https://ec.europa.eu/energy/sites/ener/files/documents/2012_energy_roadmap_2050_en_0.pdf

Evans, R. and Kay, T. (2008). "How environmentalists 'greened' trade policy: Strategic action and the architecture of field overlap," *American Sociological Review*, 73: 970–991.

Fineman, S. (1997). "Constructing the green manager," *British Journal of Management*, 8(1): 31–38.

Fineman, S. and Clarke, K. (1996). "Green stakeholders: Industry interpretations and response," *Journal of Management Studies*, 33(6): 715–731.

Fischer, K. and Schot, J. (1993). Environmental Strategies for Industry (Washington DC: Island Press).

Fleischmann, M., Beullens, P., Bloemhof-Ruwaard, J. and Van Wassenhove, L. (2001). "The impact of product recovery on logistics network design," *Production and Operations Management*, 18: 156–173.

Fligstein, N. (1997). "Social skill and institutional theory," *American Behavioral Scientist* 40: 397–405.

Forbes, L. and Jermier, J. (2002). "The institutionalization of voluntary organizational greening and the ideals of environmentalism: Lessons about official culture from symbolic organizational theory," in A. Hoffman and M. Ventresca (eds.), *Organizations, Policy and the Natural Environment: Institutional and Strategic Perspectives* (Stanford, CA: Stanford University Press): 194–213.

Freeman, E. (1984). *Strategic Management: A Stakeholder Approach* (Boston: Harper and Row).

Frosch, R. and Gallopouos, N. (1989). "Strategies for manufacturing," *Scientific American*, 261(3): 94–102.

Fullerton, J. (2015). *Regenerative Capitalism: How Universal Principles and Patterns Will Shape the New Economy* (Greenwich, CT: The Capital Institute).

Garud, R., Gehman, J. and Karnøe, P. (2010). "Categorization by association: Nuclear technology and emission-free electricity," *Research in the Sociology of Work*, 21: 51–93.

Geels, F. (2004). "From sectoral systems of innovation to socio-technical systems: Insights about dynamics and change from sociology and institutional theory," *Research Policy*, 33(6/7): 897–920.

Geertz, C. (1973). *The Interpretation of Cultures* (New York, NY: Basic Books).

Georg, S. (1994). "Regulating the environment: Changing from constraint to gentle coercion," *Business Strategy & the Environment*, 3(2): 11–20.

Georg, S. (1999). "The social shaping of household consumption," *Ecological Economics*, 28(3): 455–466.

Georg, S. and Hoffman, A. (eds.). (2013). *Business and the Environment: Critical Perspectives in Business and Management, Volumes I–IV* (Oxford, UK: Routledge).

Georg, S. and Irwin, A. (2002). "Re-interpreting local-global partnerships," in T. de Bruijn and A. Tukker (eds.), *Partnership and Leadership – Building Alliances for a Sustainable Future* (Dordrecht: Kluwer Academic Publishers): 61–76.

Georg, S. and Justesen, L. (2017). "Counting to zero: Accounting for a Green Building", *Accounting, Auditing & Accountability Journal*, 30(5): 1065–1081.

Gershoff, A. and Irwin, J. (2012). "Why not choose green? Consumer decision making for environmentally friendly products," in P. Bansal and A. Hoffman (eds.), *The Oxford Handbook on Business and the Natural Environment* (Oxford, UK: Oxford University Press): 366–383.

Gersick, C. (1991). "Punctuated equilibrium: A multi-level exploration of revolutionary change theories," *Academy of Management Review*, 16: 10–36.

Geyer, R., Van Wassenhove, L. and Atasu, A. (2007). "The economics of remanufacturing under limited component durability and finite product life cycles," *Management Science*, 53(1): 88–100.

Gibbard, P. and Walker, J. (2014). "The term 'Anthropocene' in the context of formal geological classification." Geological Society, London, Special Publications, 395: 29–37.

Gillings, M. and Hagan-Lawson, E. (2014). "The cost of living in the Anthropocene," *Earth Perspectives*, 1: 2.

Glachant, M. (1994). "The setting of voluntary agreements between industry and government: Bargaining and efficiency," *Business Strategy & the Environment*, 3(2): 43–49.

Gladwin, T. (1993). "The meaning of greening: A plea for organizational theory," in K. Fischer and J. Schot (eds.), *Environmental Strategies for Industry: International Perspectives on Research Needs and Policy Implications* (Washington, DC: Island Press): 37–61.

Gladwin, T. (2012). "Capitalism critique: Systemic limits on business harmony with nature," in P. Bansal and A. Hoffman (eds.), *The Oxford Handbook on Business and the Natural Environment* (Oxford, UK: Oxford University Press): 657–674.

Gladwin, T., Kennelly, J. and Krause, T. (1995). "Shifting paradigms for sustainable development: Implications for management theory and research," *Academy of Management Review*, 20: 874–907.

Gladwin, T., Newburry, W. and Reiskin, E. (1997). "Why is the northern elite mind biased against community, the environment, and a sustainable future," in M. Bazerman, D. Messick, A. Tenbrunsel, and K. Wade-Benzoni (eds.), *Environment, Ethics, and Behavior: The Psychology of Environmental Valuation and Degradation* (San Francisco, CA: The New Lexington Press): 234–274.

Gladwin, T. and Welles, J. (1976). "Multinational corporations and environmental protection: Patterns of organizational adaptation," *International Studies of Management and Organization*, 6(1–2): 160–184.

Gonzalez, C. (2001). "Beyond eco-imperialism: An environmental justice critique of free trade," *Denver University Law Review*, 78(4): 979–1016.

Gram-Hanssen, K. (2010). "Residential heat comfort practices: Understanding users," *Building Research and Information*, 38(2): 175–186.

Gray, R. (1992). "Accounting and environmentalism: An exploration of the challenge of gently accounting for accountability, transparency and sustainability," *Accounting, Organizations and Society*, 17(5): 399–425.

Gray, R., Bebbington, K., Walters, D. and Thomson, I. (1995). "The greening of enterprise: An exploration of the (non) role of environmental accounting and environmental accountants in organisational change," *Critical Perspectives on Accounting*, 6(3): 211–239.

Gray, R., Kouhy, R. and Lavers, S. (1995). "Corporate social and environmental reporting: A review of the literature and a longitudinal study of UK disclosure," *Accounting, Auditing and Accountability Journal*, 8(2): 47–77.

Greer, J. and Bruno, K. (1996). *Greenwash: The Reality Behind Corporate Environmentalism* (New York: Apex Press).

Hahn, R. and Stavins, R. (1991). "Incentive-based environmental regulation: A new era from an old idea," *Ecology Law Quarterly*, 18: 1–42.

Hajer, M. (1996). "Ecological modernisation as cultural politics." in S. Lash, B. Szerzynzki and B. Wynne (eds.), *Risk, Environment and Modernity: Towards a New Ecology* (London: Sage Publications): 246–268.

Hajer, M. (1997). *The Politics of Environmental Discourse: Ecological Modernization and the Policy Process* (Oxford: Oxford University Press).

Hamari, J., Sjöklint, M. and Ukkonen, A. (2016). "The sharing economy: Why people participate in collaborative consumption," *Journal of the Association for Information Science and Technology*, 67(9): 2047–2059.

Harrison, J., Bosse, D. and Harrison, R. (2010). "Managing for stakeholders, stakeholder utility functions, and competitive advantage," *Strategic Management Journal*, 31(1): 58–74.

Hart, S. (1995). "A natural-resource-based view of the firm," *Academy of Management Review*, 20(4): 986–1014.

Hart, S. (1997). "Beyond greening: Strategies for a sustainable world," *Harvard Business Review*, 75: 66–76.

Hart, S. (2007) *Capitalism at the Crossroads: Aligning Business, Earth, and Humanity* (Philadelphia, PA: Wharton School Publishing).

Hart, S. and Dowell, G. (2011). "Invited editorial: A natural-resource-based view of the firm: Fifteen years after," *Journal of Management*, 37(5): 1464–1479.

Hart, S. and Milstein, M. (1999). "Global sustainability and the creative destruction of industries," *Sloan Management Review*, 41(1): 23–33.

Hawken, P. (1993). *The Ecology of Commerce: A Declaration of Sustainability* (New York: Harper Collins).

Henn, R. and Hoffman, A. (2013). *Constructing Green: The Social Structures of Sustainability* (Cambridge, MA: MIT Press).

Henriques, I. and Sadorsky, P. (1996). "The determinants of an environmentally responsive firm: An empirical approach," *Journal of Environmental Economics and Management*, 30(3): 381–395.

Henriques, I. and Sadorsky, P. (1999). "The relationship between environmental commitment and managerial perceptions of stakeholder importance," *Academy of Management Journal*, 42(1): 87–99.

Hertwich, E. (2005). "Life cycle approaches to sustainable construction: A critical review," *Environmental Science and Technology*, 39(13): 4673–4684.

Hettige, H., Huq, M., Pargal, S. and Wheeler, D. (1996). "Determinants of pollution abatement in developing countries: Evidence from South and Southeast Asia," *World Development*, 24(12): 1891–1904.

Hilary, R. (2004). "Environmental management systems in the smaller enterprise," *Journal of Cleaner Production*, 12(6): 561–569.

Hoffman, A. (1999). "Institutional evolution and change: Environmentalism and the US chemical industry," *Academy of Management Journal*, 42(4): 351–371.

Hoffman, A. (2000) *Competitive Environmental Strategy: A Guide to the Changing Business Landscape* (Washington DC: Island Press).

Hoffman, A. (2001a). *From Heresy to Dogma: An Institutional History of Corporate Environmentalism* (Stanford, CA: Stanford University Press).

Hoffman, A. (2001b). "Linking organizational and field-level analyses: The diffusion of corporate environmental practice," *Organization & Environment*, 14(2): 133–156.

Hoffman, A. (2005). "Climate change strategy: The business logic behind voluntary greenhouse gas reductions," *California Management Review*, 47(3): 21–46.

Hoffman, A. (2011a). "The culture and discourse of climate skepticism," *Strategic Organization*, 9(1): 77–84.

Hoffman, A. (2011b). "Talking past each other? Cultural framing of skeptical and convinced logics in the climate change debate." *Organization & Environment*, 24(1): 3–33.

Hoffman, A. (2011c). "Thirty-five years of research on business and the natural environment. Part 1: A statistical synopsis," *Organizations and the Natural Environment Blog*, July 13. http://oneaomonline.blogspot.com/2011/07/thirty-five-years-of-research-on.html, Accessed on October 2, 2012.

Hoffman, A. (2015). *How Culture Shapes the Climate Change Debate* (Palo Alton, CA: Stanford University Press).

Hoffman, A. (2017). "The evolving focus of business sustainability education," in *Earth Ed: Rethinking Education on a Changing Planet* (Washington, DC: Island Press): 279–288.

Hoffman, A. and Bansal, P. (2012). "Retrospective, perspective and prospective: Introduction," in P. Bansal and A. Hoffman (eds.), *The Oxford Handbook on Business and the Natural Environment* (Oxford, UK: Oxford University Press): 3–28.

Hoffman, A. and Ehrenfeld, J. (1998). "Corporate environmentalism, sustainability and management studies," in N. Roome (ed.), *Environmental Strategies for Industry: The Future of Corporate Practice* (Washington, DC: Island Press): 55–73.

Hoffman, A. and Ehrenfeld, J. (2015). "The fourth wave: Business management and business education in the age of the Anthropocene," in E. Lawler, S. Mohrman and J. O'Toole (eds.), *Corporate Stewardship: Organizing for Sustainable Effectiveness* (Sheffield, UK: Greenleaf Publishing): 228–246.

Hoffman, A. and Haigh, N. (2011). "Positive deviance for a sustainable world: Linking sustainability and positive organizational scholarship," in Kim Cameron and Gretchen Spreitzer (eds.), *Handbook of Positive Organizational Scholarship* (Oxford, UK: Oxford University Press): 953–964.

Hoffman, A. and Jennings, P. D. (2011). "The BP oil spill as a cultural anomaly? Institutional context, conflict and change," *Journal of Management Inquiry*, 20(2): 100–112.

Hoffman, A. and Jennings, P. D. (2015). "Institutional theory and the natural environment: Research in (and on) the Anthropocene," *Organization & Environment*, 28(1): 8–31.

Hoffman, A. and Ocasio, W. (2001) "Not all events are attended equally: Toward a middle-range theory of industry attention to external events," *Organization Science*, 12: 414–434.

Hopwood, A. (2009). "Accounting and the environment," *Accounting, Organizations and Society*, 34(3–4): 433–439.

Hörisch, J., Freeman, R. E. and Schaltegger, S. (2014). "Applying Stakeholder Theory in Sustainability Management," *Organization & Environment*, 27(4): 328–346.

Howard-Grenville, J. (2006). "Inside the 'black box': How organizational culture and subcultures inform interpretations and actions on environmental issues," *Organization & Environment*, 19(1): 46–73.

Howard-Grenville, J. and Hoffman, A. (2003). "The importance of cultural framing to the success of social initiatives in business," *Academy of Management Executive*, 17(2): 70–84.

Hulme, M. (2009). *Why We Disagree About Climate Change: Understanding Controversy, Inaction and Opportunity* (Cambridge: Cambridge University Press).

Hunt, C., and Auster, E. (1990). "Proactive environmental management: Avoiding the toxic trap," *Sloan Management Review*, 31(2): 7–18.

Hunter, T. and Bansal, P. (2006). "How standard is standardized MNC global environmental communication?" *Journal of Business Ethics*, 71(2): 135–147.

Jacobs, M. (1993). *The Green Economy: Environment, Sustainable Development and the Politics of the Future* (Vancouver, BC: UBC Press).

Jacobsen, N. (2006). "Industrial symbiosis in Kalundborg, Denmark: A quantative assessment of economic and environmental aspects," *Journal of Industrial Ecology*, 10(1–2): 239–255.

Jamison, A., Eyerman, R. and Cramer, J. (1990). *The Making of the New Environmental Consciousness: A Comparative Study of the Environmental Movements in Sweden, Denmark and the Netherlands* (Edinburgh, Scotland: Edinburgh University Press).

Jänicke, M., Binder, M. and Mönch, H. (1997). "Dirty industries: Patterns of change in industrial countries," *Environmental and Resource Economics*, 9(4): 467–491.

Jänicke, M. and Jacob, K. (2004). "Lead markets for environmental innovations: a new role for the nation state." *Global Environmental Politics*, 4(1): 29–46.

Javorcik, B. and Wei, S. (2005). "Pollution havens and foreign direct investment: Dirty secret or popular myth?" *Contributions to Economic Analysis & Policy*, 3(2): 1538–0645.

Jennings, P. and Zandbergen, P. (1995). "Ecologically sustainable organizations: An institutional approach," *Academy of Management Review*, 20(4): 1015–1052.

Jeppesen, S. and Hansen, M. (2004). "Environmental upgrading of Third World enterprises through linkages to transnational corporations. Theoretical perspectives and preliminary evidence," *Business Strategy & the Environment*, 13(4): 261–274.

Jermier, J. and Forbes, L. (2003). "Greening organizations: Critical issues," in M. Alvesson and H. Willmott (eds.), *Studying Management Critically* (London: Sage Publications): 157–176.

Justesen, L. and Mouritsen, M. (2009). "The triple visual: Translations between photographs, 3-D visualizations and calculations," *Accounting, Auditing & Accountability Journal*, 22(6): 973–990.

Kallio, T. and Nordberg, P. (2006). "The evolution of organizations and natural environment discourse: Some critical remarks," *Organization & Environment*, 19(4): 439–457.

Karnøe, P. and Garud, R. (2012). "Path creation: Agency and co-creation of heterogeneous resources during the emergence of the Danish wind turbine cluster," *European Planning Studies*, 20(5): 733–752.

Kassinis, G. and Vafeas, N. (2006). "Stakeholder pressures and environmental performance," *Academy of Management Journal*, 49: 145–159.

Kemp, R. (1993). "An economic analysis of clean technology," in K. Fischer and J. Schot (eds.), *Environmental Strategies for Industry: International Perspectives on Research Needs and Policy Implications* (Washington, DC: Island Press): 79–113.

Kemp, R., Schot, J. and Hoogma, R. (1998). "Regime shifts to sustainability through processes of niche formation: The approach of strategic niche management," *Technology Analysis and Strategic Management*, 10(2): 175–198.

Kemp, R. and Soete, L. (1992). "The greening of technological progress: An evolutionary perspective," *Futures*, 25(5): 437–457.

Khanna, M. and Anton, W. (2002). "Corporate environmental management: Regulation and market based incentives," *Land Economics*, 78(4): 539–558.

Kilbourne, W. and Beckmann, S. (1998). "Review and critical assessment of research on marketing and the environment," *Journal of Marketing Management*, 14(6): 513–532.

King, A. and Lenox, M. (2000). "Industry self-regulation without sanctions: The chemical industry's responsible care program," *Academy of Management Journal*, 43(4): 698–716.

King, A. and Lenox, M. (2001a). "Does it really pay to be green? An empirical study of firm environmental and financial performance," *Journal of Industrial Ecology*, 5(1): 105–116.

King, A. and Lenox, M. (2001b). "Lean and green? An empirical examination of the relationship between lean production and environmental performance," *Production and Operations Management*, 10(3): 244–256.

King, A., Lenox, M. and Terlaak, A. (2005). "The strategic use of decentralized institutions: Exploring certification with the ISO 14001 management standard," *Academy of Management Journal*, 48: 1091–1106.

King, B. (2008) "A political mediation model of corporate response to social movement activism," *Administrative Science Quarterly*, 53: 395–421.

Klassen, R. and Whybark, D. (1999). "The impact of environmental technologies on manufacturing performance," *Academy of Management Journal*, 40(6): 599–615.

Kolk A., Levy, D. and Pinkse, J. (2008). "Corporate responses in an emerging climate regime: The institutionalization and commensuration of carbon disclosure," *European Accounting Review*, 17(4): 719–745.

Kolk, A. and Pinske, J. (2004). "Market strategies for climate change," *European Management Journal*, 22(3): 304–314.

Kong, N., Salzmann, O., Steger, U. and Ionescu-Sommers, A. (2002). "Moving business/industry towards sustainable consumption: The role of NGOs," *European Management Journal*, 20(2): 109–127.

Koplin, J., Seuring, S. and Mesterham, M. (2007). "Incorporating sustainability into supply chain management in the automotive industry – the case of Volkswagen AG," *Journal of Cleaner Production*, 15(11–12): 1053–1062.

Koppenjan, J. F. M. and Enserink, B. (2009). "Public-private partnerships in Urban Infrastructures: Reconciling private sector participation and sustainability," *Public Administration Review*, 69(2): 284–296.

Korten, D. (1995). *When Corporations Rule the World* (Bloomfield, CT: Kumarian Press Inc.).

Kostova, T., Roth, K. and Dacin, M. (2008). "Institutional theory in the study of multinational corporations," *Academy of Management Review*, 33(4): 994–1006.

Kostova, T. and Zaheer, S. (1999). "Organizational legitimacy under conditions of complexity: The case of the multinational enterprise," *Academy of Management Review*, 24(1): 64–81.

Krabbe, O., Linthorst, G., Blok, K., Crijns-Graus, W., van Vuuren, D. P., Höhne, N., Faria, P., Aden, N. and Pineda, A. C. (2015). Aligning corporate greenhouse-gas emissions targets with climate goals. *National Climate Change*, 5, 1057–1060.

Kraemer, J. and Gostin, L. (2012). "The limits of government regulation of science," in *Georgetown Law Faculty Publications and Other Works*, 776. http://scholarship.law.georgetown.edu/facpub/

Kubliszewski, I., Costanza, R., Franco, C., Lawn, P., Talberth, J., Jackson, T. and Aylmer, C. (2013) "Beyond GDP: Measuring and achieving global genuine progress," *Ecological Economics*, 93: 57–68.

Kuhn, T. (1970). *The Structure of Scientific Revolutions* (Chicago, IL: The University of Chicago Press).

Labatt, S. and Maclaren, V. (1998). "Voluntary corporate environmental initiatives: A typology and preliminary investigation," *Environment and Planning C: Government and Policy*, 16(2): 191–209.

Latour, B. (1987). *Science in Action* (Cambridge, MA: Harvard University Press).

Latour, B. (1998). "To modernize or to ecologize? That is the question," in B. Braun and N. Castree (eds.), *Remaking Reality* (London: Routledge): 221–242.

Latour, B. (2004). *Politics of Nature: How to Bring the Sciences into Democracy*, trans. Porter C. (Cambridge, MA: Harvard University Press).

Latour, B. (2013). *Facing Gaia: Six Lectures on the Political Theology of Nature* (Gifford Lectures on Natural Religion, February 2013). www.bruno-latour. fr/sites/default/files/downloads/GIFFORD-ASSEMBLED.pdf. Accessed on August 23, 2017.

Law, J. (1992). "Notes on the theory of the actor-network: ordering, strategy, and heterogeneity," *Systemic Practice and Action Research*, 5(4): 379–393.

Lawrence, T. (1999). "Institutional strategy," *Journal of Management*, 25: 161–188.

Lawrence, T. and Phillips, N. (2004). "From Moby Dick to Free Willy: Macrocultural discourse and institutional entrepreneurship in emerging institutional fields," *Organization*, 11: 689–711.

Lee, W. H. and Moscardo, G. (2005). "Understanding the impact of ecotourism resort experiences on tourists' environmental attitudes and behavioural intentions." *Journal of Sustainable Tourism*, 13(6): 546–565.

Lefsrud, L. and Meyer, R. (2012). "Science or science fiction? Professionals' discursive construction of climate change," *Organization Studies*, 33(1):1477–1506.

Lenox, M. and King, A. (2004). "Prospects for developing absorptive capacity through internal information provision," *Strategic Management Journal*, 25(4): 331–345.

Lenox, M. and Nash, J. (2003). "Industry self-regulation and adverse selection: A comparison across four trade association programs," *Business Strategy & the Environment*, 12(6): 343–356.

Lenzen, M. (2000). "Errors in conventional and input-output-based life-cycle inventories," *Journal of Industrial Ecology*, 4(4): 127–148.

Levy, D. (1997). "Environmental management as political sustainability," *Organization & Environment*, 10(2): 126–147.

Levy, D. and Kolk, A. (2002). "Strategic responses to global climate change: Conflicting pressures on multinationals in the oil industry," *Business and Politics*, 4(3): 275–300.

Lewandowski, M. (2016). "Designing the business models for circular economy – towards the conceptual framework," *Sustainability*, 8(1): 43; doi:10.3390/su8010043

Lifset, R. (2008). "The quantitative and qualitative in industrial ecology," *Journal of Industrial Ecology*, 12(2):133–135.

Lohmann, L. (2005). "Marketing and making carbon dumps: Commodification, calculation and counterfactuals in climate change mitigation", *Science as Culture*, 14, 203–235.

London, T. (2016). *The Base of the Pyramid Promise: Building Businesses with Impact and Scale* (Palo Alto, CA: Stanford University Press).

London, T. and Hart, S. (2004). "Reinventing strategies for emerging markets: Beyond the transnational model," *Journal of International Business Studies*, 35: 350–370.

Lounsbury, M. (2001). "Institutional sources of practice variation: Staffing college and university recycling programs," *Administrative Science Quarterly*, 46: 29–56.

Lovbrand, E. et al. (2015). "Who speaks for the future of the Earth? How critical social science can extend the conversation on the Anthropocene," *Global Environmental Change*, 32: 211–218.

Lovelock, J. (1972). "Gaia as seen through the atmosphere." *Atmospheric Environment*, 6: 579–580.

Lovelock, J. (2000). *Gaia: A New Look at Life on Earth* (Oxford, UK: Oxford University Press).

Lyon, T. and Maxwell, J. (2011). "Greenwash: Corporate environmental disclosure under threat of audit," *Journal of Economics and Management Strategy*, 20(1): 3–41.

MacKenzie, D. (2006). An Engine, Not a Camera: How Financial Models Shape Markets (Cambridge, MA: MIT Press).

Mackenzie, D. (2009). "Making things the same: Gases, emission rights and the politics of carbon markets," *Accounting, Organizations and Society*, 34(3–4): 440–455.

MacKenzie, D. and Millo, Y. (2003). "Constructing a market, performing theory: The historical sociology of a financial derivatives exchange", *American Journal of Sociology*, 109: 107–145.

Macnaghten, P. and Urry, J. (1998). *Contested Natures* (London: Sage Publications).

Maguire, S., Hardy, C. and Lawrence, T. (2004). "Institutional entrepreneurship in emerging fields: HIV/AIDS treatment advocacy in Canada," *Academy of Management Journal*, 47: 657–679.

Maquire, S. and Hardy, C. (2009). "Discourse and deinstitutionalization: The decline of DDT," *Academy of Management Journal*, 52: 148–178.

March, J. (1991). "Exploration and exploitation in organizational learning," *Organization Science*, 2(1): 71–87.

March, J. (2007). "The study of organizations and organizing since 1945," *Organization Studies*, 28(1): 9–19.

Margolis, J. and Walsh, J. (2003). "Misery loves companies: Rethinking social initiatives by business," *Administrative Science Quarterly*, 48(2): 268–305.

Markussson, N. (2010). "The championing of environmental improvements in technology investment projects," *Journal of Cleaner Production*, 18(8): 777–783.

Matten, D. and Crane, A. (2005). "Corporate citizenship: Toward an extended theoretical conceptualization," *Academy of Management Review*, 30(1): 166–179.

Matten D. and Moon, J. (2008) "'Implicit' and 'explicit' CSR: A conceptual framework for a comparative understanding of corporate social responsibility," *Academy of Management Review*, 33(2): 404–424.

McDonough, W. and Braungart, M. (2013). *The Upcycle: Beyond Sustainability – Designing for Abundance* (New York, NY: North Point Press).

Meadows, D., Meadows, D., Randers, J. and Behrens, W. (1972). *The Limits to Growth* (New York: Universe Books).

Melville, N. (2012). "Information systems, business and the natural environment: Can digital business transform environmental sustainability?" in P. Bansal and A. Hoffman (eds.), *The Oxford Handbook on Business and the Natural Environment* (Oxford, UK: Oxford University Press): 327–345.

Meyer, R. and Boxenbaum, E. (2010). "Exploring European-ness in organization research," *Organization Studies*, 31(6): 737–755.

Min, H. and Galle, W. (1997). "Green purchasing strategies: Trends and implications," *International Journal of Purchasing and Materials Management*, 33(3): 10–17.

Mitchell, R., Agle, B. and Wood, D. (1997). "Toward a theory of stakeholder identification and salience: Defining the principle of who and what really counts," *Academy of Management Review*, 22: 853–886.

Morsing, M. (2006). "Corporate social responsibility as strategic auto-communication: On the role of external stakeholders for member identification," *Business Ethics: A European Review*, 15(2): 171–182.

Nehrt, C. (1998). "Maintainability of first mover advantages when environmental regulations differ between countries," *Academy of Management Review*, 23(1): 77–97.

Neu, D., Warsame, H. and Pedwell, K. (1998). "Managing public impressions: Environmental disclosures in annual reports," *Accounting, Organizations and Society*, 23(3): 265–282.

Newton, T. (2002). "Creating the new ecological order? Elias and actor-network theory," *Academy of Management Review*, 27(4): 523–540.

Newton, T. and Harte, G. (1997). "Green business: Technicist kitsch?" *Journal of Management Studies*, 34(1): 75–98.

Nidumolu, R., Prahalad, C. K. and Rangaswami, M. R. (2009). "Why sustainability is now the key driver of innovation," *Harvard Business Review*, September, 2–9.

Nyberg, D. and Wright, C. (2016). "Performative and political: Corporate constructions of climate change risk," *Organization*, 23(5): 617–638.

Oldfield, F. et al. (2014) "The Anthropocene review: Its significance, implications and the rationale for a new transdisciplinary journal," *The Anthropocene Review*, 1(1): 3–7.

Organization for Economic Cooperation and Development (OECD). (2000). *Innovation and the Environment* (OECD: Paris).

Organization for Economic Cooperation and Development (OECD). (2003). *Voluntary Approaches for Environmental Policy: Effectiveness, Efficiency and Usage in Policy Mixes* (Paris: OECD).

Orlitzky, M., Schmidt, F. and Rynes, S. (2003). "Corporate social and financial performance: A meta-analysis," *Organization Studies*, 24(3): 403.

Orsato, R. and Clegg, S. (1999). "The political ecology of organizations: Toward a framework for analyzing business-environment relationships," *Organization & Environment*, 12(3): 263–279.

Orsato, R., den Hond, F. and Clegg, S. (2002). "The political ecology of automobile recycling in Europe," *Organization Studies*, 23(4): 639–665.

Owyang, J., Tran, C. and Silva, C. (2013). *The Collaborative Economy* (San Mateo, CA: The Altimeter Group).

Paterson, M., Humphreys, D. and Pettiford, L. (2003). "Conceptualizing global environmental governance: From inter-state regimes to counter-hegemonic struggles," *Global Environmental Policy*, 3(2):1–10.

Peattie, K. (2001). "Towards sustainability: The third age of green marketing," *Marketing Review*, 2 (Winter): 129.

Pedersen, E. R. and Neergaard, P. (2006). Caveat empto – let the buyer beware: Environmental labeling and the limitations of green consumerism," *Business Strategy & the Environment*, 15(1): 15–29.

Perrow, C. (2010). "Organisations and global warming," in *Handbook of Society and Climate Change* (London: Routledge).

Petts, J., Herd, A., Gerrad, S. and Homes, C. (1999). "The climate and culture of environmental compliance in SMEs," *Business Strategy & the Environment*, 8(1): 14–30.

Porter, M. (1991, April). "America's green strategy," *Scientific American*, 264(4): 168.

Porter, M. and Van Der Linde, C. (1995). "Green and competitive: Ending the stalemate," *Harvard Business Review*, September–October: 120–134.

Post. J. and Altman, B. (1992). "Models of corporate greening: How corporate social policy and organizational learning inform leading-edge environmental management," *Research in Corporate Social Performance and Policy*, 3: 3–29.

Potoski, M. and Prakash, A. (2004). "The regulation dilemma: Cooperation and conflict in environmental governance," *Public Administration Review*, 64(2): 152–163.

Prahalad, C. K. and Hart, S. (2002). "The fortune at the bottom of the pyramid," *Strategy & Business*, 26(1st quarter): 54–67.

Prakash, A. and Kellman, K. (2004). "Policy modes, firms and the natural environment," *Business Strategy & the Environment*, 13(2): 107–128.

Pregger, T., Nitsch, J. and Naegler, T. (2013). "Long-term scenarios and strategies for the deployment of renewable energies in Germany," *Energy Policy*, 59: 350–360.

Qinghua, Z. and Sarkis, J. (2004). "Relationships between operational practices and performance among early adopters of green supply chain management practices in Chinese manufacturing enterprises," *Journal of Operations Management*, 22(3): 265–289.

Ramus, C. and Steger, U. (2000). "The roles of supervisory support behaviors and environmental policy in employee 'ecoinitiatives' at leading-edge European companies," *Academy of Management Journal*, 43(4): 605–626.

Randalls, S. (2010). "Weather profits: Weather derivatives and the commercialization of meteorology," *Social Studies of Science*, 40(5): 705–730.

Reid, E. and Toffel, M. (2009). "Responding to public and private politics: Corporate disclosure of climate change strategies," *Strategic Management Journal*, 30: 1157–1178.

Reinhardt, F. (1998). "Environmental product differentiation: Implications for corporate strategy," *California Management Review*, 40(4): 43–73.

Reinhardt, F. (1999). "Market failure and the environmental policies of firms: Economic rationales for 'beyond compliance' behavior," *Journal of Industrial Ecology*, 3(1): 9–21.

Reverdy, T. (2006). "Translation process and organizational change: ISO 14001 implementation," *International Studies of Management and Organization*, 36(2): 9–30.

Rivera, J. and deLeon, P. (2005). "Chief executive officers and voluntary environmental performance: Costa Rica's certification for sustainable tourism," *Policy Sciences*, 38(2): 417–437.

Rockström, J. et al. (2009). "Planetary boundaries: Exploring the safe operating space for humanity," *Ecology and Society*, 14(2): 32.

Roome, N. (ed.). (1998). *Sustainability Strategies for Industry: The Future of Corporate Practice* (Washington, DC: Island Press).

Roome, N. (2012). "Looking back, thinking forward: Distinguishing between weak and strong sustainability," in P. Bansal and A. Hoffman (eds.), *The Oxford Handbook of Business and the Natural Environment*, (Oxford, UK: Oxford University Press): 620–629.

Røpke, I. (2017). "Sustainability and the governance of the financial system: What role for full reserve banking?" *Environmental Policy and Governance*, 27: 177–192.

Røpke, I., Christensen, T. and Jensen, O. (2010). "Information and communication technologies – a new round of household electrification," *Energy Policy*, 38(4): 1764–1773.

Rowan, R. (2014). "Notes on politics after the Anthropocene," in E. Johnson and H. Morehouse (eds.), "After the Anthropocene: Politics and geographic inquiry for a new epoch," *Progress in Human Geography*, 38, 9–12.

Russell, S., Milne, M. J. and Dey, C. (2017). "Accounts of nature and the nature of accounts: Critical reflections on environmental accounting and propositions for ecologically informed accounting," *Accounting, Auditing & Accountability Journal*, 30(7): 1426–1458.

Russo, M. and Fouts, P. (1997). "A resource-based perspective on corporate environmental performance and profitability," *Academy of Management Journal*, 40: 534–559.

Russo, M. and Minto, A. (2012). "Competitive strategy and the environment: A field of inquiry emerges," in P. Bansal and A. Hoffman (eds.), *The Oxford Handbook of Business and the Environment* (Oxford: Oxford University Press): 29–49.

Sandelands, L. and Hoffman, A. (2008). "Sustainability, faith and the market," *Worldviews: Global Religions, Culture and Ecology*, 12: 129–145.

Sarkis, J. (2003). "A strategic decision framework for green supply chain management," *Journal of Cleaner Production*, 11(4): 397–409.

Schatzki, T., Cetina, K. and von Savigny, E. (2001). *The Practice Turn in Contemporary Theory* (London: Routledge).

Schmidheiny, S. (1992). *Changing Course: A Global Business Perspective on Development and the Environment* (Cambridge, MA: MIT Press).

Schnaiberg, A. (1980). *The Environment: From Surplus to Scarcity* (New York: Oxford University Press).

Schot, J. (1992). "Constructive technology assessment and technological dynamics: The case of clean technology," *Technology and Human Values*, 17(1): 36–56.

Schumpeter, J. (1994) [1942]. *Capitalism, Socialism and Democracy* (London, UK: Routledge).

Sexton, K., Marcus, A., Easter, W. and Burkhardt, T. (eds.). (1999). *Better Environmental Decisions: Strategies for Governments, Businesses and Communities* (Washington, DC: Island Press).

Sharfman, M., Shaft, T. and Tihanyi, L. (2004). "A model of the global and institutional antecedents of high-level corporate environmental performance," *Business and Society*, 43(1): 6–36.

Sharma, P. (2004). "An overview of the field of family business studies: Current status and directions for the future," *Family Business Review*, 17(1): 1–36.

Sharma, S. (2000). "Managerial interpretations and organizational context as predictors of corporate choice of environmental strategy," *Academy of Management Journal*, 43: 681–697.

Sharma, S. and Henriques, I. (2005). "Stakeholder influences on sustainability practices in the Canadian forest products industry," *Strategic Management Journal*, 26: 159–180.

Sharma, S. and Vredenburg, H. (1998). "Proactive corporate environmental strategy and the development of competitively valuable organizational capabilities," *Strategic Management Journal*, 19(8): 729–753.

Short, J. L. and Toffel, M. W. (2010). "Making self-regulation more than merely symbolic: The critical role of the legal environment," *Administrative Science Quarterly*, 55: 361–396.

Shove, E. (2003). *Comfort, Cleanliness and Convenience. The Social Organization of Normality* (Oxford: Berg).

Shove, E., Chappells, H., Lutzenhiser, L. and Hackett, B. (2008). "Comfort in a lower carbon society," *Building Research and Information*, 36(4): 307–311.

Shove, E. and Pantzar, M. (2005). "Consumers, producers and practices. Understanding the invention and reinvention of Nordic walking," *Journal of Consumer Culture*, 5(1): 43–64.

Shove, E. and Walker, G. (2010). "Governing transitions in the sustainability of everyday life," *Research Policy*, 39(4): 471–476.

Shrivastava, P. (1987). "Preventing industrial crises: The challenges of Bhopal," *International Journal of Mass-Emergencies and Disasters*, 5(3): 199–221.

Shrivastava, P. (1994). "Castrated environment: Greening organizational studies," *Organization Studies*, 15: 705–726.

Shrivastava, P. (1995a). "Environmental technologies and competitive advantage," *Strategic Management Journal*, 16: 183–200.

Shrivastava, P. (1995b) "The role of corporations in achieving environmental sustainability," *Academy of Management Review*, 20(4): 936–960.

Siegel, D. (2009). "Green management matters only if it yields more green: An economic strategic perspective," *Academy of Management Perspectives*, 23(3): 5–16.

Sine, W., Haveman, H. and Tolbert, P. (2005). "Risky business? Entrepreneurship in the new independent power sector," *Administrative Science Quarterly*, 50: 200–232.

Sine, W. and Lee, B. (2009) "Tilting at windmills? The environmental movement and the emergence of the U.S. wind energy sector," *Administrative Science Quarterly*, 54: 123–155.

Smith, A., Stirling, A. and Berkhout, F. (2005). "The governance of sustainable socio-technical transitions," *Research Policy*, 34: 1491–1510.

Smith, D. and Brown, M. (2003). "Sustainability and corporate evolution: Integrating vision and tools at Norm Thompson Outfitters," *Journal of Organizational Excellence*, 22(4): 3–14. 3

Springett, D. (2003). "Business conceptions of sustainable development: A perspective from critical theory," *Business Strategy & the Environment*, 12(2): 71–86.

Srivastava, S. K. (2007). "Green supply-chain management: A state-of-the-art literature review," *International Journal Management Reviews*, 9(1): 53–80.

Starik, M. (1995). "Should trees have managerial standing? Toward stakeholder status for non-human nature," *Journal of Business Ethics*, 14: 207–217.

Starik, M. and Kanashiro, P. (2013). "Toward a theory of sustainability management: Uncovering and integrating the nearly obvious," *Organization & Environment*, 26(1): 7–30.

Starik, M. and Marcus, A. (2000). "Introduction to the special research forum on the management of organizations in the natural environment: A field emerging from multiple paths, with many challenges ahead," *Academy of Management Journal*, 43(4): 539–546.

Starik, M. and Rands, G. (1995). "Weaving an integrated web: Multilevel and multi-system perspectives of ecologically sustainable organizations," *Academy of Management Review*, 20(4): 908–935.

Stead, E. and Stead, J. (1995). *Management for a Small Planet* (London: Sage Publications).

Steffen, W., Broadgate, W., Deutsch, L., Gaffney, O. and Ludvig, C. (2015). "The trajectory of the Anthropocene: The great acceleration," *The Anthropocene Review*, 2(1): 81–98.

Steffen, W., Crutzen, P. and McNeil, J. (2007). "The Anthropocene: Are humans overwhelming the great forces of nature?" *AMBIO*, 36(8): 614–621.

Stengers, I. (2015). *In Catastrophic Times: Resisting the Coming Barbarism*, trans. Goffey, A. (Ann Arbor, MI: Open Humanities Press).

Sterman, J. (2012). "Sustaining sustainability: Creating a systems science in a fragmented academy and polarized world," in M. Weinstein and R. Turner (eds.), *Sustainability Science: The Emerging Paradigm and the Urban Environment* (New York: Springer): 21–58.

Stern, N. (2009). *The Global Deal: Climate Change and the Creation of a New Era of Progress and Prosperity* (New York: Public Affairs).

Stiglitz, J. (2009). *Freefall: Free Markets and the Sinking of the Global Economy* (London: Penguin Books).

Stiglitz, J., Sen, A. and Fitoussi, J. (2015). *Mismeasuring Our Lives: Why GDP Doesn't Add Up* (New York, NY: The New Press).

Stockholm Resilience Center. (2016). *Planetary Boundaries – an Update*, www.stockholmresilience.org/research/research-news/2015-01-15-planetary-boundaries---an-update.html.

Stoudt, L. (2012). *The Problem of Corporate Purpose* (Washington, DC: Brookings Institution).

Suddaby, R. and Greenwood, R. (2005). "Rhetorical strategies of legitimacy," *Administrative Science Quarterly*, 50: 35–67.

Taylor, D. (2000). "The rise of the environmental justice paradigm: Injustice framing and the social construction of environmental discourses," *American Behavioral Scientist*, 43(4): 508–580.

Terlaak, A. and King, A. (2006). "The effect of certification with the ISO 9000 Quality Management Standard: A signaling approach," *Journal of Economic Behavior and Organization*, 60(4): 579–602.

Thierry, M., Salomon, M., Van Nunen, J. and Van Wassenhove, L. N. (1995). "Strategic issues in product recovery management," *California Management Review*, 37(2): 114–135.

Toffel, M. (2006). "Resolving information asymmetries in markets: The role of certified management programs," Harvard Business School Working Paper, No. 07–023.

Touboulic, A. and Walker, H. (2015). "Theories in sustainable supply chain management: A structured literature review," *International Journal of Physical Distribution & Logistics Management*, 45(1/2): 16–42.

United Nations Sustainable Development Goals (UNSDG). (2017). www.un.org/sustainabledevelopment/news/press-releases/.

Unruh, G. (2000). "Understanding carbon lock-in," *Energy Policy*, 28(12): 817–830.

Urhammer, E., & Røpke, I. (2013). "Macroeconomic narratives in a world of crises: An analysis of stories about solving the system crisis," *Ecological Economics*, 96: 62–70.

Utting, P. (2005). "Corporate responsibility and the movement of business," *Development in Practice*, 15(3–4): 375–389.

Vachon, S. and Klassen, R. (2006). "Extending green practices across the supply chain: The impact of upstream and downstream integration," *International Journal of Operations and Production Management*, 26(7): 795–821.

Van Hoek, R. (1999). "From reversed logistics to green supply chains," *Supply Chain Management*, 4(3): 129–134.

Vogel, D. (2005) *The Market for Virtue: The Potential and Limits of Corporate Social Responsibility* (Washington, DC: Brookings Institution Press).

Waddock, S. and Graves, S. (1997). "The corporate social performance-financial performance link," *Strategic Management Journal*, 18: 303–319.

Wade-Benzoni, K. and Tost, L. (2009). "The egoism and altruism of intergenerational behavior," *Personality and Social Psychology Review*, 13: 165–193.

Walker, H., Sisto, L. and McBain, D. (2008). "Drivers and barriers to environmental supply chain management practices: Lessons from the public and private sectors," *Journal of Purchasing and Supply Management*, 14(1): 69–85.

Walley, N. and Whitehead, B. (1994). "It's not easy being green," *Harvard Business Review*, 72(3): 46–52.

Walls, J. and Hoffman, A. (2012). "Exceptional boards: Environmental experience and positive deviance from institutional norms," *Journal of Organizational Behavior*, 34(2): 253–271.

Walton, S., Handfield, R. and Melnyk, S. (1998). "The green supply chain: Integrating suppliers into environmental management processes," *International Journal of Purchasing and Materials Management*, 34(2): 2–11.

Wapner, P. (1995). "Politics beyond the state: Environmental activism and world civic politics," *World Politics*, 47: 311–340.

Warde, A. (2005) "Consumption and theories of practice," *Journal of Consumer Culture*, 5(2): 131–153.

Wasserman, S. and Faust, K. (1994). *Social Network Analysis: Methods and Applications* (Cambridge: Cambridge University Press).

Weber, K., Heinze, K. and Desoucey, M. (2008). "Forage for thought: Mobilizing codes in the movement for grass-fed meat and dairy products," *Administrative Science Quarterly*, 53: 529–567.

Webster, K. (2015). *The Circular Economy: A Wealth of Flows* (Cowes, UK: Ellen MacArthur Foundation).

Weick, K. (1995). *Sensemaking in Organizations* (Thousand Oaks, CA: Sage Publications, Inc).

Welford, R. (ed.). (1997). *Hijacking Environmentalism: Corporate Response to Sustainable Development* (London: Earthscan).

Wernick, I., and Ausubel, J. (1995). "National material flows and the environment," *Annual Review of Energy and the Environment*, 20(1): 463–492.

Whiteman, G. and Cooper, W. (2000). "Ecological embeddedness," *Academy of Management Journal*, 43(6): 1265–1282.

Whiteman, G., Parker, J., Kennedy, S. and Williams, A. (Forthcoming). "Dealing with grand challenges: Using science-based boundary objects for cross- organizational sensemaking," *Science, Technology & Human Values*.

Whiteman, G., Walker, B. and Perego, P. (2013) "Planetary boundaries: Ecological foundations for corporate sustainability," *Journal of Management Studies*, 50(2): 307–336.

Wood, D. (1991). "Corporate social performance revisited," *Academy of Management Review*, 16(4): 691–718.

World Commission on Environment and Development (WCED). (1987). *Our Common Future* (Oxford, UK: Oxford University Press).

Wright, C. and Nyberg, D. (2015). *Climate Change, Capitalism and Corporations: Processes of Creative Self-Destruction* (Cambridge, UK: University of Cambridge Press).

Wright, C. and Nyberg, D. (2016). "An inconvenient truth: How organizations translate climate change into business as usual," *Academy of Management Journal*. 60(5): 1633–1661: doi: 10.5465/amj.2015.0718.

Yearly, S. (1992) "Green ambivalence about science: Legal-rational authority and the scientific legitimation of a social movement," *British Journal of Sociology*, 43: 511–532.

Young, S. B. (2015). "Responsible sourcing of metals: Certification approaches for conflict minerals and conflict-free metals," *The International Journal of Life Cycle Assessment*, 1–19.

Zalasiewicz, J., Williams, M., Steffen, W. and Crutzen, P. (2010). "The new world of the Anthropocene," *Environment Science & Technology*, 44(7): 2228–2231.

Zamagni, A., Masoni, P., Buttol, P., Raggi, A. and Buonamici, R. (2012). "Finding life cycle assessment research direction with the aid of meta-analysis," *Journal of Industrial Ecology*, 16: S39–S52.

Zhu, Q., Lowe, E., Wei, Y.-A. and Barnes, D. (2007). "Industrial symbiosis in China: A case study of the Guitang Group," *Journal of Industrial Ecology*, 11(1): 31–42.

Zhu, Q. and Sarkis, J. (2004). "Relationships between operational practices and performance among early adopters of green supply chain management practices in Chinese manufacturing enterprises," *Journal of Operations Management*, 22(3): 265–289.

Zsidisin, G. and Siferd, S. (2001). "Environmental purchasing: A framework for theory development," *European Journal of Purchasing and Supply Management*, 7(1): 61–73.

Appendix I
258 Journals in which B&NE research was published between 1975–2010

Accounting

Non-Specialized: *ACCA Research Report; Accounting and Business Research; Accounting Forum; Accounting Horizons; Accounting Review; Accounting, Auditing and Accountability Journal; Advances in Environmental Accounting and Management; Advances in Public Interest Accounting; Australian Accounting Review; British Accounting Review; Chartered Accountants Journal of New Zealand; Contemporary Accounting Research; Critical Perspectives on Accounting; European Accounting Review; International Journal of Accounting; International Journal of Accounting Information Systems; Irish Accounting Review; Journal of Accounting and Economics; Journal of Accounting and Public Policy; Journal of Accounting Literature; Journal of Accounting Research; Journal of Accounting, Auditing and Finance; Pacific Accounting Review; Research on Accounting Ethics; Review of Accounting Studies*

Specialized: *Accounting, Organizations and Society; Attitudes and Environmentally-Sensitive Accounting; Social and Environmental Accountability Journal*

Behavior: psychology, sociology, organizational behavior

Non-Specialized: *American Behavioral Scientist; American Journal of Sociology; American Sociological Review; Annual Review of Sociology; Basic and Applied Social Psychology; British Journal of Sociology; Cultural Anthropology; Human Resource Management; Journal of Applied Behavioral Science; Journal of Applied Psychology; Journal of Experimental Social Psychology; Journal of Organizational Change Management; Journal of Organizational Excellence; Journal*

of Personality and Social Psychology; Organization; Organization Science; Organization Studies; Organizational Behavior and Human Decision Processes; Psychological Science; Research in Organizational Behavior; Rural Sociology; Sociologia Ruralis; Sociological Inquiry; Sociological Perspectives; Sociological Theory
Specialized: *Journal of Environmental Psychology; Organization & Environment*

Economics

Non-Specialized: *American Economic Review; Comparative Economic Studies; Contemporary Economic Policy; Contributions to Economic Analysis and Policy; Development; Economic Geography; Economic Inquiry; Empirical Economics; Energy Journal; Energy Policy; Forest Policy and Economics; Journal of Agricultural and Food Industrial Organization; Journal of Development Economics; Journal of Economic Behavior and Organization; Journal of Economic Literature; Journal of Economic Perspectives; Journal of Economics and Management Strategy; Land Economics; Major Themes in Economics; RAND Journal of Economics; Review of Economics and Statistics; Small Business Economics; Socio-Economic Review; Southern Economic Journal; The BE Journal of Economic Analysis and Policy; Topics in Economic Analysis*

Specialized: *Ecological Economics; Environmental and Resource Economics; Frontiers of Environmental Economics; International Yearbook of Environmental and Resource Economics; Journal of Agricultural and Resource Economics; Journal of Environmental Economics and Management; Resource and Energy Economics*

Engineering/science/environment

Non-Specialized: *Building Research and Information; Computers and Industrial Engineering; Issues in Science and Technology; Nature; Science; Transactions of the Institute of British Geographers; FINANCE; European Financial Management; Financial Analysts Journal; Financial Management; Financial Services Review; Journal of Banking and Finance; Journal of Behavioral Finance; Journal of Corporate Finance; Journal of Financial and Quantitative Analysis; Journal of Financial Economics; Journal of Investing*

Specialized: *Annual Review of Energy and the Environment; Annual Review of Environment and Resources; Annual Review of*

Environmental Resources; Climatic Change; Environmental Pollution; Environmental Science and Technology; Journal of Industrial Ecology

Information systems

Non-Specialized: *MIS Quarterly*

Law

Non-Specialized: *Administrative Law Review; American Business Law Journal; Duke Environmental Law and Policy Forum; Harvard Environmental Law Review; Journal of Criminal Law and Criminology; Journal of Law and Economics; Journal of Law, Economics and Organization; Law and Policy; University of Pennsylvania Law Review; Yale Law Journal*

Specialized: *Ecology Law Quarterly; Environmental Law Reporter; Stanford Environmental Law Journal; UCLA Journal of Environmental Law and Policy*

Management

Non-Specialized: *Academy of Management Journal; Academy of Management Learning and Education; Academy of Management Review; Administrative Science Quarterly; Benchmarking: An International Journal; British Journal of Management; British Management Journal; Business History Review; Business Horizons; Canadian Journal of Administrative Sciences-Revue Canadienne Des Sciences De L Administration; Columbia Journal of World Business; Cornell Hotel and Restaurant Administration Quarterly; Corporate Governance; Corporate Reputation Review; Decision Sciences; Decision Support Systems; Emergence: Complexity and Organization; European Management Journal; Family Business Review; Global Business and Organizational Excellence; Growth and Change; Interfaces; International Business Review; International Entrepreneurship Management Journal; International Journal of Management Reviews; International Studies of Management and Organization; Journal of American Academy of Business; Journal of Business Research; Journal of Business Strategy; Journal of Business Venturing; Journal of International Business Studies; Journal of International Management; Journal of Management; Journal of Management Studies;*

Journal of Managerial Issues; Journal of Risk and Uncertainty; Long Range Planning; Management Decision; Management Research News; Management Science; Strategic Management Journal; Strategic Organization; Technology Analysis and Strategic Management; Transnational Corporations

Specialized: *Business and Society; Business and Politics; Business Ethics Quarterly; Business Strategy & the Environment; Corporate Environmental Strategy; Corporate Social Responsibility and Environmental Management; Corporate Social Responsibility and Human Rights; Environment and Planning; Environmental Education Research; Environmental Management; Environmental Performance; Global Environmental Change; Greener Management International; Industrial and Environmental Crisis Quarterly; International Journal of Environment and Sustainable Development; International Journal of Sustainable Development; Journal of Business Ethics; Journal of Corporate Citizenship; Journal of Environmental Management; Journal of Environmental Planning and Management; Research in Corporate Social Performance and Policy; Resources, Conservation, and Recycling; Society and Natural Resources; Sustainable Development; Journal of Cleaner Production*

Marketing

Non-Specialized: *Advances in Consumer Research; European Journal of Marketing; Industrial Marketing Management; Journal of Academy of Marketing Science; Journal of Advertising; Journal of Business and Industrial Marketing; Journal of Communication Management; Journal of Consumer Affairs; Journal of Consumer Marketing; Journal of Consumer Policy; Journal of Consumer Psychology; Journal of Consumer Research; Journal of Macromarketing; Journal of Marketing; Journal of Marketing Management; Journal of Marketing Theory and Practice; Journal of Strategic Marketing; Marketing Intelligence and Planning; Marketing Review; Qualitative Market Research: An International Journal*

Operations

Non-Specialized: *Business Process Management Journal; European Journal of Purchasing and Supply Management; Industrial Management and Data Systems; International Journal of Operations and Production Management; International Journal of Physical Distribution* and Logistics Management; International Journal of Production and Operations Management; International Journal of Production Economics; International Journal of Production Research; International Journal of Purchasing and Materials Management; Journal of Operations Management; Journal of Purchasing and Supply Management; Journal of Supply Chain Management; Operations Research; Production and Operations Management; Supply Chain Management; Systems Dynamics Review; Transportation Research Part E, Logistics and Transportation Review

Political science

Non-Specialized: *American Journal of Political Science; British Journal of Political Science; International Journal of Public Administration; International Studies Quarterly; Journal of Comparative Policy Analysis: Research and Practice; Journal of Policy Analysis and Management; Journal of Political Economy; Journal of Politics; Journal of Public Administration Research and Theory; Journal of Public Economics; Journal of Public Policy and Marketing; New Political Economy; Oxford Review of Economic Policy; Policy Sciences; Policy Studies Journal; Public Administration Review; Regional Studies; Regulation and Governance; Research Policy; Social Forces; Social Problems; World Politics; Zeitschrift für Umweltpolitik*
Specialized: *Environmental Politics; Journal of Environmental Assessment Policy and Management*

Professional

Non-Specialized: *Academy of Management Executive; California Management Review; Harvard Business Review; New York Times; New York Times Magazine; Sloan Management Review; Stanford Social Innovation Review; Technology Review; Technovation*
Specialized: *Total Quality Environmental Management; EPA Journal; Waste Management*

Appendix II

Representative papers in the B&NE field

Article Title	HistCite File Code	Google Scholar Citation Count	Citations Per Year
Gladwin T. and Welles, J. (1976). "Multinational corporations and environmental protection: Patterns of organizational adaptation," *International Studies of Management and Organization*, 6(1–2): 160–184.	N1*	28	0.8
Carroll, A. (1979). "A three-dimensional conceptual model of corporate performance," *Academy of Management Review*, 4: 497–505	N2	2048	62.1
Hahn, R. and Stavins, R. (1991) "Incentive-based environmental regulation: A new era from an old idea," *Ecology Law Quarterly*, 18(1): 1–42.	1	431	20.5
Wood D. (1991) "Corporate social performance revisited," *Academy of Management Review*, 16(4): 691–718.	2	1566	74.6
Gray, R. (1992). "Accounting and environmentalism: An exploration of the challenge of gently accounting for accountability, transparency and sustainability," *Accounting, Organizations and Society*, 17(5): 399–425.	3	324	16.2
Yearly, S. (1992). "Green ambivalence about science: Legal-rational authority and the scientific legitimation of a social movement," *British Journal of Sociology*, 43: 511–532.	4	58	2.9

Note: *Articles noted by N are not in the HistCite database

(*Continued*)

Article Title	HistCite File Code	Google Scholar Citation Count	Citations Per Year
Gladwin, T. (1993). "The meaning of greening: A plea for organizational theory," in K. Fischer and J. Schot (eds.), *Environmental Strategies for Industry: International Perspectives on Research Needs and Policy Implications* (Washington, DC: Island Press): 37–61.	N3	157	8.3
Clarkson, M. (1995). "A stakeholder framework for analyzing and evaluating corporate social performance," *Academy of Management Review*, 20: 92–117.	5	1979	116.4
Thierry et al., 1995). "Strategic issues in product recovery management," *California Management Review*, 37(2): 114–35.	6	568	33.4
Starik, M. (1995). "Should trees have managerial standing? Toward stakeholder status for non-human nature," *Journal of Business Ethics*, 14: 207–217.	7	175	10.3
Wapner, P. (1995). "Politics beyond the state: Environmental activism and world civic politics," *World Politics*, 47: 311–340.	8	933	54.9
Shrivstava, P. (1995a). "Environmental technologies and competitive advantage," *Strategic Management Journal*, 16: 183–200.	9	405	23.8
Gladwin, T., Kennelly, J. and Krause, T. (1995). "Shifting paradigms for sustainable development: Implications for management theory and research," *Academy of Management Review*, 20: 874–907.	10	628	36.9
Starik, M. and Rands, G. (1995). "Weaving an integrated web: Multilevel and multisystem perspectives of ecologically sustainable organizations," *Academy of Management Review*, 20(4): 908–935.	11	347	20.4

(*Continued*)

Article Title	HistCite File Code	Google Scholar Citation Count	Citations Per Year
Shrivstava, P. (1995a). "The role of corporations in achieving environmental sustainability," *Academy of Management Review*, 20 (4): 936–960.	12	514	30.2
Hart, S. (1995). "A natural-resource-based view of the firm," *Academy of Management Review*, 20(4): 986–1014.	13	1229	72.3
Jennings, P. D. and Zandbergen, P. (1995). "Ecologically sustainable organizations: An institutional approach," *Academy of Management Review*, 20(4): 1015–1052.	14	296	17.4
Porter, M. and van der Linde, C. (1995). "Toward a new conception of the environment-competitiveness relationship," *Journal of Economic Perspectives*, 94: 97–118.	15	1850	108.8
Egri, C. and Pinfield, L. (1996). "Organizations and the biosphere: Ecologies and environments," In S. Clegg, C. Hardy, and W. Nord (eds.), *Handbook of Organization Studies* (London: Sage Publications): 459–483.	N4	96	6.0
Henriques, I. and Sadorsky, P. (1996). "The determinants of an environmentally responsive firm: An empirical approach," *Journal of Environmental Economics and Management*, 30(3): 381–395.	16	401	25.1
Ehrenfeld, J. and Gertler, N. (1997). "Industrial ecology in practice: The evolution of interdependence at Kalundborg," *Journal of Industrial Ecology*, 1(1): 67–79.	N5	231	15.4
Hart, S. (1997). "Beyond greening: Strategies for a sustainable world," *Harvard Business Review*, 75: 66–76.	17	817	54.5
Waddock, S. and Graves, S. (1997). "The corporate social performance-financial performance link," *Strategic Management Journal*, 18: 303–319.	18	1132	75.5

(*Continued*)

Article Title	HistCite File Code	Google Scholar Citation Count	Citations Per Year
Russo, M. and Fouts, P. (1997). "A resource-based perspective on corporate environmental performance and profitability," *Academy of Management Journal*, 40: 534–559.	19	1092	72.8
Mitchell, R., Agle, B. and Wood, D. (1997). "Toward a theory of stakeholder identification and salience: Defining the principle of who and what really counts," *Academy of Management Review*, 22: 853–886.	20	2635	175.7
Kemp, R., Schot, J. and Hoogma, R. (1998). "Regime shifts to sustainability through processes of niche formation: The approach of strategic niche management," *Technology Analysis and Strategic Management*, 10(2): 175–198.	21	527	37.6
Reinhardt, F. 1998). "Environmental product differentiation: Implications for corporate strategy," *California Management Review*, 40(4): 43–73.	22	177	12.6
Sharma, S. and Vredenburg, H. (1998). "Proactive corporate environmental strategy and the development of competitively valuable organizational capabilities," *Strategic Management Journal*, 19(8): 729–53.	23	602	43.0
Henriques, I. and Sadorsky, P. (1999). "The relationship between environmental commitment and managerial perceptions of stakeholder importance," *Academy of Management Journal*, 42: 87–99.	24	452	34.8
Georg, S. (1999). "The social shaping of household consumption," *Ecological Economics*, 28: 455–466.	25	44	3.4
Hoffman, A. (1999). "Institutional evolution and change: Environmentalism and the US chemical industry," *Academy of Management Journal*, 42(4): 351–371.	26	662	50.9

(*Continued*)

Article Title	HistCite File Code	Google Scholar Citation Count	Citations Per Year
Egri, C. and Herman, S. (2000). "Leadership in the North American environmental sector: Values, leadership styles, and contexts of environmental leaders and their organizations," *Academy of Management Journal*, 43(4): 571–604.	27	213	17.8
Christmann, P. (2000). "Effects of 'best practices' on environmental management on cost advantage: The role of complementary assets," *Academy of Management Journal*, 43(4): 663–680.	28	374	31.2
Sharma, S. (2000). "Managerial interpretations and organizational context as predictors of corporate choice of environmental strategy," *Academy of Management Journal*, 43: 681–697.	29	441	36.8
King, A. and Lenox, M. (2000). "Industry self-regulation without sanctions: The chemical industry's Responsible Care program," *Academy of Management Journal*, 43(4): 698–716.	30	632	52.7
Bansal, P. and Roth, K. (2000) "Why companies go green: A model of ecological responsiveness," *Academy of Management Journal*, 43: 717–736.	31	634	52.8
Klassen, R. and Whybark, D. (1999). "The impact of environmental technologies on manufacturing performance," *Academy of Management Journal*, 40(6): 599–615.	32	348	26.8
Christmann, P. and Taylor, G. (2001). "Globalization and the environment: Determinants of firm self-regulation in China," *Journal of International Business Studies*, 32(3): 439–458.	33	267	24.3

(*Continued*)

Article Title	HistCite File Code	Google Scholar Citation Count	Citations Per Year
King, A. and Lenox, M. (2001a). "Does it really pay to be green? An empirical study of firm environmental and financial performance," *Journal of Industrial Ecology*, 5(1): 105–116.	34	253	23.0
Lounsbury, M. (2001). "Institutional sources of practice variation: Staffing college and university recycling programs," *Administrative Science Quarterly*, 46: 29–56.	35	199	18.1
Banerjee, S. (2001). "Managerial perceptions of corporate environmentalism: Interpretations from industry and strategic implications for organizations," *Journal of Management Studies*, 38(4): 489–513.	36	124	11.3
Hoffman, A. (2001b). "Linking organizational and field-level analyses: The diffusion of corporate environmental practice," *Organization & Environment*, 14(2): 133–156.	37	129	11.7
Corbett C. and Kirsch, D. (2001). "International diffusion of ISO 14000 certification," *Production and Operations Management*, 10(3): 327–342.	38	134	12.2
Delmas, M. (2002). "The diffusion of environmental management standards in Europe and in the United States: An institutional perspective," *Policy Sciences*, 35(1): 91–119.	39	153	15.3
Georg, S. and Irwin, A. (2002) "Re-interpreting local-global partnerships," in T.de Bruijn and A. Tukker (eds.) *Partnership and Leadership – Building Alliances for a Sustainable Future* (Kluwer Academic Publishers, Dordrecht): 61–76.	N6	1	0.1

(*Continued*)

Appendix II (Continued)

Article Title	HistCite File Code	Google Scholar Citation Count	Citations Per Year
Sarkis, J. (2003). "A strategic decision framework for green supply chain management," *Journal of Cleaner Production*, 11(4): 397–409.	40	194	21.6
Aragón-Correa, J. and Sharma, S. (2003). "A contingent resource-based view of proactive corporate environmental strategy," *Academy of Management Review*, 28(1): 71–88.	41	313	34.8
Bhattacharya, C. B. and Sen, S. (2003). "Consumer-company identification: A framework for understanding consumers' relationships with companies," *Journal of Marketing*, 67(4): 76–88.	42	378	42.0
Margolis, J. and Walsh, J. (2003). "Misery loves companies: Rethinking social initiatives by business," *Administrative Science Quarterly*, 48(2): 268–305.	43	799	88.8
Bansal, P. (2003) "From issues to actions: The importance of individual concerns and organizational values in responding to natural environmental issues," *Organization Science*, 14: 510–527.	44	113	12.6
Bansal, P. and Clelland, I. (2004). "Talking trash: Legitimacy, impression management, and unsystematic risk in the context of the natural environment," *Academy of Management Journal*, 47(1): 197–218.	45	153	19.1
Ehrenfeld, J. (2004) "Searching for sustainability: No quick fix," *Reflections*, 5(8): 1–13	N7	31	3.9
Jeppesen S. and Hansen, M. (2004). "Environmental upgrading of Third World enterprises through linkages to transnational corporations. Theoretical perspectives and preliminary evidence," *Business Strategy & the Environment*, 13(4): 261–274.	N8	20	2.5

(*Continued*)

Appendix II (Continued)

Article Title	HistCite File Code	Google Scholar Citation Count	Citations Per Year
Kolk, A. and Pinske, J. (2004). "Market strategies for climate change," *European Management Journal*, 22(3): 304–314.	N9	113	14.1
London, T and Hart, S. (2004). "Reinventing strategies for emerging markets: Beyond the transnational model," *Journal of International Business Studies*, 35: 1–21.	46	297	37.1
Matten, D. and Crane, A. (2005). "Corporate citizenship: Toward an extended theoretical conceptualization," *Academy of Management Review*, 30(1): 166–179.	47	328	46.9
Smith, A., Stirling, A. and Berkhout, F. (2005). "The governance of sustainable socio-technical transitions," *Research Policy*, 34: 1491–1510.	48	246	35.1
Vachon, S. and Klassen, R. (2006). "Extending green practices across the supply chain: The impact of upstream and downstream integration," *International Journal of Operations and Production Management*, 26(7): 795–821.	49	72	12.0
Howard-Grenville, J. (2006). "Inside the 'black box': How organizational culture and subcultures inform interpretations and actions on environmental issues," *Organization & Environment*, 19: 46–73.	50	37	6.2
Barnett, M. and Salomon, R. (2006). "Beyond dichotomy: The curvilinear relationship between social responsibility and financial performance," *Strategic Management Journal*, 27(11): 1101–1122.	51	124	20.7
Aguilera et al. (2007). "Putting the S back in Corporate Social Responsibility: A multi-level theory of social change in organizations," *Academy of Management Review*, 32(3): 836–863.	52	256	51.2

(Continued)

Article Title	HistCite File Code	Google Scholar Citation Count	Citations Per Year
Banerjee, S. (2008). "Corporate social responsibility: The good, the bad and the ugly," *Critical Sociology*, 34(1): 51–79.	53	157	39.3
Darnall, N. and Sides, S. (2008). "Assessing the performance of voluntary environmental programs: Does certification matter?" *Policy Studies Journal*, 36(1): 95–117.	54	38	9.5
Matten D., and Moon, J. (2008). "'Implicit' and 'explicit' CSR: A conceptual framework for a comparative understanding of corporate social responsibility," *Academy of Management Review*, 33(2): 404–424	55	196	49.0
Weber, K., Heinze, K. and Desoucey, M. (2008) "Forage for thought: Mobilizing codes in the movement for grass-fed meat and dairy products," *Administrative Science Quarterly*, 53: 529–567.	56	41	10.3
Maquire, S. and Hardy, C. (2009). "Discourse and deinstitutionalization: The decline of DDT," *Academy of Management Journal*, 52: 148–178.	57	33	11.0
Sine, W. and Lee, B. (2009) "Tilting at windmills? The environmental movement and the emergence of the U.S. wind energy sector," *Administrative Science Quarterly*, 54: 123–155.	58	26	8.7
Mackenzie, D. (2009). "Making things the same: Gases, emission rights and the politics of carbon markets," *Accounting, Organizations and Society*, 34(3–4): 440–455.	59	69	23.0
Nidumolu, R., Prahalad, C.K. and Rangaswami, M. (2009). "Why sustainability is now the key driver of innovation," *Harvard Business Review*, September: 4–10.	60	51	17.0
Shove, E. and Walker, G. (2010). "Governing transitions in the sustainability of everyday life," *Research Policy*, 39(4): 471–476	61	21	10.5

Index

Page numbers in italics indicate figures and page numbers in bold indicate tables.